Killer Kids
Volume Eight
22 Shocking
True Murder Cases

Robert Keller

Please Leave Your Review of This Book At
http://bit.ly/kellerbooks

ISBN: 9798488995970

© 2021 by Robert Keller

robertkellerauthor.com

Table of Contents

Nathan Brooks

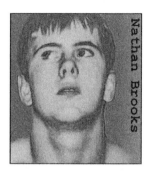

In the run-up to Halloween 1995, 17-year-old Nathan Brooks made a boast to his classmates at Bellaire High School, in Belmont County, Ohio. "Come Saturday, I'm going to be famous," he announced without preamble. No one took him seriously. Nathan was not the kind of kid who attracted much attention. He was a middling student who stayed out of trouble and kept mostly to himself. If he was going to live up to his boast, one of his fellow students joked, he would have to "pull off another Wickliffe." This was a reference to a shooting that had occurred at a middle school in Wickliffe, Ohio, less than a year earlier, in which one person was killed and five injured.

And perhaps more attention should have been paid to that flippantly delivered jibe. Because, while Nathan Brooks was not planning a school shooting, he *was* planning a massacre. An avowed Satanist, he had compiled a list of 16 names, all of them targets for sacrificial murder. The first three slots on that list were occupied by his brother Ryan and by his parents, Terry and

Marilynn. The date on which he planned to carry out the killings was Friday, September 29, 1995.

Ryan Brooks, 16-year-old younger brother of the aforementioned Nathan, attended a school football game that evening. Later, he went to the home of his friend Erik, where he hung out until after midnight. Finally, at around 1:30 a.m., Ryan called home, intending to ask his father if he could spend the night. Except that it wasn't his father who answered the phone. It was his big brother, Nathan.

"Tell mom and dad that I'm staying the night at Erik's house," Ryan told him. To this, Nathan responded that Ryan should return home, that their father was already pissed at him for being out past curfew, that he shouldn't get himself deeper into trouble than he already was. Ryan's response was that he might sleep over anyway and deal with the consequences in the morning. Then he hung up, staying another hour before he decided that he probably should take his brother's advice. He then asked Erik for a ride home.

That sequence of teenaged rebellion, followed by contrition, most probably saved Ryan his life. While Ryan was hanging out with his friend Erik, a slaughter was taking place at the Brooks residence, the likes of which Ryan could never have imagined. Nathan Brooks, middling student and secret Satanist, was laying claim to his 15 minutes of celebrity, writing his name in the bloody pantheon of teenaged killers. At some point during that evening, Nathan entered his parents' bedroom, armed with an array of weapons.

Terry Brooks died first, shot three times in the head at close range with a hunting rifle. Then Nathan turned on his mother, hacking and stabbing her to death with the knife and ax he'd brought with him. Finally, with both of his parents dead, he fetched a hacksaw from the garage and used it to cut off his father's head. This he placed in a punchbowl, which he arranged on a chair in the living room. He then sat down to wait for his brother to get home. It was Ryan's call at 1:30 in the morning that threw him off his plan. At first, he sat waiting, hoping for Ryan's return. Eventually, growing impatient, he set off to fetch his brother from Erik's house. If the victim wouldn't come to him, he would go to the victim.

It was here that Ryan's decision to return home likely saved his life. The brothers must have passed each other on route because when Nathan arrived at Erik's house, Ryan had already left. Erik's mother was miffed to be roused from her bed at this hour and also somewhat uneasy at Nathan's demeanor. He appeared disheveled, breathless, slightly manic. She told him that his brother wasn't there and then closed the door in his face.

Ryan, meanwhile, had arrived home. Entering quietly through the kitchen, he was dismayed to see splatters of blood on the floor. He then walked to the living room where he was met by the horrific sight of his father's decapitated head, grotesquely displayed in the punchbowl. That the young man did not turn and flee at this point is a testimony to his courage. Instead, he searched the house, finding blood everywhere. His father's decapitated corpse lay in the master bedroom, arms raised above his torso in a parody of surrender. His mother was on the adjacent twin bed, partially covered by a blood-soaked comforter, the handle of a long-bladed knife protruding from her right side. There were deep gashes to her head and face, apparently inflicted by the bloody ax that lay at the foot of the bed. Turning away from this gruesome scene, Ryan ran for the phone and dialed 911.

At first, the police were concerned for Nathan's safety, worried that he too might have fallen victim to the as-yet-unidentified killer. But a search of the teenager's room quickly changed his status from potential victim to possible suspect. An alert went out, and it did not take long to find Nathan. He was sitting pensively among the gravestones at the local cemetery, his hands still caked with the dried blood of his parents. He offered no resistance when he was taken into custody and said nothing to either confirm or deny his involvement in the murders.

In the aftermath of the dreadful events of September 30, few in Bellaire could comprehend the motive behind the murders. One person who did understand was Ryan Brooks. He knew that his brother had substance abuse problems and had been using drugs and alcohol; he knew that Nathan was indulging in animal cruelty and dabbling in Satanism. Nathan had once described Satan to him as "my best friend." What Ryan could not have known was the extent of his brother's madness nor the breadth of his ambition. Evidence found at the crime scene suggested that Nathan Brooks had planned to slaughter at least sixteen individuals.

This evidence would later be presented at Nathan Brooks' trial. It was in the form of a journal that included various satanic sketches and also a list of people who had been targeted for murder. Top of the list was Ryan. Positions two and three were occupied by the killer's parents, Terry and Marilynn. Four more names were identified as relatives of the Brooks family while another name was that of a local priest. Next to some of the entries, Nathan had written additional notes to himself. Eviscerate. Decapitate. Dismember. Molest. Skin. Crucify. Those whose names were on the list could be glad that Nathan Brooks was safely in police custody.

One of the immediate consequences of the Brooks murders was the cancellation of Halloween. The killings had sent shockwaves across the communities of the Ohio Valley and there were widespread fears that Brooks might not have been operating alone, that there might be other Satanists in their midst, just waiting to strike. In Bellaire, councilors took the extraordinary step of banning trick-or-treating. The last thing they needed was hordes of kids wandering the darkened streets. It was decided instead to host an alternative event at a local green space. Dubbed "Boo at the Park," it is a tradition that endures to this day. Decades later, Nathan Brooks still casts a long shadow over the town.

But Brooks is safely locked away now, serving a life sentence that will keep him behind bars until at least 2038. A jury of six men and six women unanimously found him guilty on two charges of aggravated murder, rejecting his insanity defense. As a teenager, Brooks had scrawled in this notebook that, "Satan will bring me peace." He will now have to find that peace in the bosom of the Ohio Department of Corrections.

Sharon Carr

The date was June 7, 1992. In the small town of Camberley, England, 18-year-old apprentice hairdresser, Katie Rackliff, was enjoying a night out, partying at a local nightclub called Ragamuffins. But this wasn't really a party for Katie. She had recently broken up with her boyfriend and was nursing a broken heart. Her evening was entirely spoiled when the object of her affection showed up at the club with his new girlfriend. Eventually, at around two in the morning, a slightly tipsy Katie decided to leave and walk home. She had covered only a short distance when a car pulled up beside her, two young men in the front, an even younger girl in the back. The girl asked if Katie wanted a ride and she accepted, getting into the backseat.

But it was soon evident to Katie that her benefactors were not taking her home, that they were going in the wrong direction. She demanded to be let out and eventually the girl, who had introduced herself as Sharon, told the driver to stop. Then Katie quickly exited the vehicle and started walking away. All thoughts of her lost love had been banished now. Her heart was racing. She felt certain that she'd just had a narrow escape from being raped...or something worse. She was still chastising herself for being stupid enough to get into the car when she was suddenly hit from behind.

Not just hit, Katie realized in an instant. She'd been cut. Pain flared in her back as the blade bit in. Desperate, she tried to turn, to right herself as she fell. But the attacker was on her now, forcing her to the ground, pinning her down. Katie was barely able to defend herself before she was stabbed in the chest. She just about had time to register that it was the girl, not one of the men, who was attacking her. Then she was stabbed again, and again, and again.

Thirty deep stab wounds would be inflicted on Katie Rackliff that night, some delivered with such force that the blade passed right through her body. She suffered massive injuries and bled out right there, on the cold, hard ground. But her killer was still not done. Lifting Katie's blouse and cutting through her bra, Sharon started mutilating her victim's breasts. Then she pulled down her jeans and used the knife to mutilate her genitals. Later, she would record in her journal, "The air stops in the back of her throat. I know all her life her breathing has worked, but it does not now. And I am joyful." Astonishingly, on the night that she murdered Katie Rackliff, on the day that she wrote this macabre testament to murder, Sharon Carr was only 12 years old.

The murder of Katie Rackliff deeply traumatized the residents of Camberley and its surrounding communities. With this level of violence, with these horrific mutilations, the police were convinced that they had a sexually sadistic psychopath on their streets, one who was very likely to kill again. A massive operation was launched to catch the killer but ultimately, it came up empty. The trail went cold. Someone had gotten away with murder.

Then, in June of 1994, almost two years to the day since Katie Rackliff's murder, the Surrey police were called to the scene of another stabbing, this one at Collingwood College in Camberley. Here, two 14-year-old schoolgirls had gotten into an altercation, and one had produced a knife and stabbed the other. The victim, Ann-Marie Clifford suffered serious but not life-threatening injuries. The attacker, Sharon Carr, was arrested and charged with causing actual bodily harm. She was later convicted and sent to Bulwood Hall Young Offenders Institution, to be detained "at Her Majesty's pleasure." There she would prove to be a problematic inmate, frequently attacking staff and other internees. She also gained a reputation as a big talker. More specifically, she liked to boast about a murder that she'd committed. Soon, rumors of this alleged killing reached the ears of the authorities.

The murder of Katie Rackliff had now gone unsolved for four years and investigators had all but given up hope of resolving it. Now here was a suspect who perhaps explained why their inquiries had come up empty. They had been hunting an adult male, one who they believed would have a record for prior sex offenses. Never in their wildest imaginings would they have suspected an adolescent girl. Never, that is, until they started reading Sharon Carr's journals.

"I am a killer," she had written. "Killing is my business and business is good. I was born to be a murderer. Killing for me is a mass turn-on and it just makes me so high I never want to come down. Every night I see the Devil in my dreams - sometimes even in my mirror, but I realize it was just me."

There were also more specific entries, which might well have been referencing the terrible death of Katie Rackliff. "I bring the knife into her chest. Her eyes are closing. She is pleading with me so I bring the knife to her again and again. I don't want to hurt her but I need to do violence to her. I need to overcome her beauty, her serenity, her security. There I see her face when she died. I know she feels her life being slowly drawn from her and I hear her gasp. I guess she was trying to breathe."

Another entry mentioned Katie by name. On 7 June, Carr had written: "Respect to Katie Rackliff. Four years today." That disclosure was enough for detectives to flag Sharon Carr as a serious suspect in the unsolved murder. They visited Carr at Bulwood Hall, subjecting her to 27 hours of interrogation. Not that Sharon was holding back. She gleefully recounted the gory details, even mentioning that she'd had sex with the two men she'd been with, after committing the murder. Her coldness, her complete lack of emotion in describing these events, left investigators stunned. Just what could have brought someone so young to such a dark place?

Sharon Carr was born in Belize in 1981 and was brought to England by her mother and stepfather. She never knew her biological father and would grow up in an unstable home, with a revolving cast of paternal figures. Her mother would have four children by three different men and would jump from one violent, abusive relationship to the next with unerring regularity. She also gave as good as she got. On one occasion, she put one of her boyfriends in the hospital. More often, though, it was she who ended up in the ER.

Growing up in the midst of such violence and discord, it is perhaps not surprising that Sharon grew to be a problem child. In fact, she became so hard to handle that her mother eventually gave her over to the authorities to be fostered. Sharon was back within a month, with no one able to control her violent mood swings. Shortly after, she kidnapped a neighbor's dog and decapitated it with a shovel. She also dropped her sister's pet hamsters into a deep fryer. During this time, Sharon's mother had absolutely no control over her 12-year-old daughter. Sharon came and went as she pleased. She stayed out until all hours, smoking, drinking, and having sex with boys. She also carried a knife, with a wicked six-inch blade, and spoke of her desire to use it on somebody. It was while out cruising on one of these nights that she encountered Katie Rackliff.

Sharon Carr was brought to trial for murder at Winchester Crown Court in December 2003. In truth, the case against her was weak, with no forensic evidence or eyewitness testimony. But for her confession and macabre diaries, there would not have been a case to answer. But Carr's performance in the dock was telling. She seemed to revel in the details of the evil that she had done. And lest there was any doubt as to her misdeeds, there were references in her journals that revealed facts only the killer would have known.

In the end, the jury had no doubt. They found Carr guilty, and she was sentenced to life in prison, with the minimum tariff set at 14 years. That was later reduced on appeal to just twelve years and opened up a frightening prospect. Sharon Carr would likely walk free while in her thirties. The chances that she would kill again were considered high by most experts.

Fortunately, Sharon Carr would turn out to be her own worst enemy. She was an extremely problematic inmate who proved almost impossible for prison officers to control. After numerous attacks on staff and other inmates, she was eventually sectioned under the Mental Health Act and transferred to Broadmoor Hospital. There she was diagnosed with schizoaffective disorder. What this means is that Carr can be held indefinitely and will only be released once the authorities are certain that she no longer poses a threat to society. Given Carr's particular brand of psychopathic rage, she is likely to remain behind bars for a very long time.

Anthony Barbaro

On the afternoon of December 30, 1974, 17-year-old Anthony Barbaro left his home in Olean, New York. Anthony was carrying a rifle as he walked out to his car but there was nothing unusual about that. He was the star marksman on his school's rifle team. He told his brother Colin that he was going to get in some shooting practice. What he failed to mention was that the targets he was going to be firing at were people.

Leaving his house at around 2:30 on that frigid afternoon, Barbaro drove to Olean High School, where he was an honor student. The school was closed for the holidays, but he managed to gain entry through an unlocked side door. He proceeded to the third floor where he took up a position at a window overlooking a busy street. Removing his rifle from its bag, he loaded it, then sighted along its barrel, drawing a bead on various pedestrians and drivers passing by. Satisfied that he had his sights in, he leaned the rifle against a wall and donned a gas mask. He then took a smoke

grenade from his rucksack and pulled the pin, causing white
smoke to begin billowing from the canister.

What Barbaro didn't realize was that there was a 12-man custodial
team performing routine maintenance at the school. Most of the
men were working in the basement but one of them, 62-year-old
Earl Metcalf, was walking the empty corridors when he noticed
smoke seeping under a door. Metcalf immediately pulled a fire
alarm and then went to investigate. He was met by Babaro,
emerging from the smoke in his mask, rifle in hand. The boy did
not hesitate, pulling the trigger and killing the custodian on the
spot. He then turned and went back to the window. With the fire
alarm clanging in the background, he leveled the rifle and took
aim. Then he started shooting.

Thirty-one shots were fired that day, the first of them directed at
pedestrians and the occupants of passing vehicles. Then
firefighters arrived in response to the alarm and Barbaro shifted
his aim and started shooting at them. Eight firemen were hit but
none of the wounds, thankfully, were fatal. Barbaro's civilian
targets had not fared as well. Neil Pilon, a 58-year-old Columbia
Gas employee was shot and killed while crossing the street;
Carmen Wright, 25, was shot in the head while driving by the
school in her car. She was six months pregnant at the time. Three
other pedestrians, including 12-year-old Julius Wright, survived
bullet wounds. Several more people sustained injuries from flying
glass fragments.

By now, the area outside the school resembled a war zone, with
police, ambulances, and even a National Guard unit having

responded to the crisis. Trapped inside the building, Anthony Barbaro had no chance of escape. Still, he refused to surrender. Eventually, it was decided to flush him out, with two police officers and four national guardsmen volunteering for the task. The men entered the building at 5:20 p.m. and soon reached the classroom where the gunman was holed up. Two tear gas canisters were tossed into the darkness and the volunteers then waited for the gas to take effect before entering. They fully expected the be met by gunfire but Barbaro was found unconscious on the floor. His defective gas mask had offered no protection from the noxious fumes. After a check confirmed that he had not suffered any injuries, he was strapped to a stretcher and carried from the school. An ambulance would provide his transport to the Olean City Jail.

The following day, December 31, 1974, Anthony Barbaro was arraigned on three counts of second-degree murder, six counts of first-degree assault, and five counts of first-degree reckless endangerment. He was ordered to be held without bond until his trial. As his identity was made public, there was a sense of disbelief among the community and particularly among the staff and students of Olean High. Anthony Barbaro made a very unlikely mass shooter.

Born in Olean in 1958, Anthony Barbaro was a lifelong resident of the town. His family was well-established in the community. Barbaro's father was an executive at a large manufacturing company while his mother managed a local fast-food chain, where Anthony also worked part-time. He was an introverted boy who did well academically and had recently been inducted into the National Honor Society. He'd also won a Regents Scholarship to

New York University, where he hoped to study engineering. According to his teachers, he was a well-behaved student who never gave them a moment of trouble. Classmates said that he was a loner although one of his teammates on the rifle team shared a story that was somewhat out of step with the general perception of Anthony Barbaro. He said that Anthony had spoken of holding up the Olean Armory and engaging the police in a standoff. Investigators would later find proof of this scheme in Barbaro's bedroom. A journal was retrieved from his closet, outlining detailed plans for the proposed shooting.

This suggests that Barbaro was planning a massacre long before the dreary December afternoon when he wreaked havoc on the unwary citizens of Olean. But it fails to answer the question of why. Why would this academically gifted boy, with no hint of trouble in his background, suddenly turn into a mass killer? The answer may be found in a "suicide note" that Barbaro left behind at the crime scene. It read: "I guess I just wanted to kill the person I hate most...myself. I just didn't have the courage. I wanted to die, but I couldn't do it, so I had to get someone to do it for me."

Unfortunately for Barbaro, his plan to commit "suicide by cop" had failed. Now he was facing the full force of the law and the prospect of a very long time in jail. In December 1975, he appeared before a judge and entered a plea of not guilty by reason of insanity. Shortly thereafter, he was transferred from the Olean City Jail to the Cattaraugus County Jail in Little Valley, New York. In October, he appeared before a grand jury at the Olean Municipal Building, where his attorney reiterated the defense stance that Barbaro suffered from "a serious, deep-rooted mental illness that precluded his conviction on murder charges." This was countermanded by two court-appointed psychiatrists who stated that Barbaro was sane and therefore competent to stand trial.

The issue of whether or not Anthony Barbaro should be held responsible for his actions would no doubt have formed the bulk of legal argument at his trial. But those arguments would never be presented in a court of law. On November 1, 1975, Barbaro was found hanging by the neck in his cell, having fashioned a bedsheet into a makeshift noose. He'd left behind a suicide note.

To whom it may concern,

People are not afraid to die, it's just how they die. I don't fear death, but rather the pain. But no more. I regret the foods I'll never taste, the music I'll never hear, the sights I'll never see, the accomplishments I'll never accomplish, in other words, I regret my life. Some will always ask, 'Why?' I don't know – no one will. What has been, can't be changed. I'm sorry. It ends like it began; in the middle of the night, someone might think it selfish or cowardly to take one's own life. Maybe so, but it's the only free choice I have. The way I figure, I lose either way. If I'm found not guilty, I won't survive the pain I've caused – my guilt. If I'm convicted, I won't survive the mental and physical punishment of my life in prison.

It was a poignant epitaph from a young man whose life had held so much promise but had, in the end, delivered nothing by destruction. Four people were dead because of his selfish actions – one of them an unborn child.

The Collie Killers

From the small town of Collie, Western Australia, comes this disturbing tale of a truly unspeakable crime, a murder devoid of motive but committed with extraordinary malice. The perpetrators of this outrage were two teenaged girls, barely 16 years old when they decided to snuff out the life of a younger friend. They were dubbed Julie and Britney by some sections of the media, although these are not their real names. Australian law prevents them from being identified. Their evil deed, though, is laid bare for all to see. This is what happened.

Britney had come to Collie via a series of unfavorable circumstances, not least her mother's three failed marriages. Britney's own father had walked out when she was just three years old, leaving her mother destitute. Struggling to make ends meet, Susan Smith had brought her family to the scruffy coal mining town of Collie, one of the few places in the state where rents were affordable to her. It was at primary school that Britney met Julie. The girls, with just four days in age between them, hit it off immediately.

Julie had endured a similarly difficult path through life. Her father had died of a drug overdose when she was four, and she'd thereafter been raised by her mother and later by a stepfather. Then, in June 2002, the family had been involved in a serious car accident that had killed her mom and left her stepbrother seriously injured. Julie had survived and so too had her stepfather,

Peter, who had taken on the task of raising her and her stepbrother. He did his best, but Julie harbored a deep-seated resentment towards him, something that she often expressed in writings on her computer. "Why did he live when my mom died?" she typed in one entry. She probably expected that no one but she would ever read it.

But someone else did read it. Peter was using his stepdaughter's computer when he discovered the writings. Julie's antagonism hurt him deeply. It irreparably damaged the relationship between them. Within six months, she'd moved out and gone to live with a school friend's family. When that arrangement didn't work out, Britney begged Susan to let Julie move in with them. Given their precarious financial position, Susan was less than keen. However, she eventually relented. Britney and Susan, who often referred to themselves as 'twins,' were now living under the same roof.

And for a time, it seemed that the relationship would be beneficial for all concerned. Julie had a home with a stable family; Britney had a friend and companion; Susan received a welfare grant to help her pay for Julie's care. However, the feeling of goodwill did not last long. In January 2004, shortly after the girls celebrated their 14th birthday, Susan's older daughter called her at work and told her that there were over a dozen kids in the house "causing havoc." Susan arrived to find a raucous party in session with blaring music and drunken, drugged-up youths. She soon ejected the group, much to the disgust of Britney and Julie. Britney would never forgive her mother for that intervention.

But while Susan had at least some control over what went on in her house, she could do little about events that happened outside. Drugs were rife among teenagers in town and both Britney and Julie soon fell into the culture. Britney was changing in other ways too, in the way she dressed, in the music she listened to, in her academic performance and school attendance. Even more frighteningly, she had begun to self-harm, with cuts running up her arms. Rightly or wrongly, Susan put much of this down to Julie's influence. By mid-2004, she'd decided that it would probably be better if Julie moved out.

Julie's next move was to a farm about 12 miles out of town, the home of another school friend. However, her new surrogate mother was soon dealing with similar problems to what Susan had endured. Julie was surly, insolent, and unresponsive. She often expressed dark thoughts and spoke frequently of suicide. Eventually, she carried through on that threat, cutting so deeply into her wrists that she had to be airlifted to a hospital in Perth, 120 miles away.

Julie would recover from her ordeal and return to the home of her 'surrogate mom.' When the woman's marriage failed and she moved from the farm into town, Julie came with her. That was bad news for Susan. Previously, there had been distance between the girls. Now that was gone and Britney fell into old habits with her friend, truanting from school, taking drugs, and hanging out with the gangs of unruly youngsters that were commonplace in Collie. Things eventually came to a head in November 2005, when Susan refused to allow one of Britney's friends to stay at the house and Britney responded by saying that she was leaving too. Over the weeks that followed, she stayed away, crashing at the houses of various friends, while Susan tried desperately to bring her home. With the police unable to help, Susan eventually turned to the Collie Family Center, which arranged for Susan and Britney to see a counselor.

Unfortunately, that session did not go as Susan had hoped. Britney insisted on speaking to the counselor alone and spun a story about being physically abused. As a result, Susan was told that Britney was being moved to a 'safe house' and that she was to have no unauthorized contact with her daughter. Susan later learned that the 'safe house' was actually a caravan parked on a social worker's front lawn. Britney shared this cramped space with another teen, 15-year-old Eliza Jane Davis.

Eliza was similar to Britney in many ways. She liked emo music, dressing in dark clothing, and writing bleak poetry. She also enjoyed doing drugs. But Eliza was different when it came to schooling. She was an academically gifted girl and seldom, if ever, missed a class. The reason she was living in the caravan was to be close to her preferred school, Collie High, which was too far to reach from either of her parents' homes.

For Susan, this was a difficult time. Separated from her daughter and worried about her wellbeing, she'd often drive around town, hoping to catch a glimpse of her. Sometimes she'd take her food, but their relationship was at a low ebb. Susan then got troubling news. Britney had been ejected from the caravan and was living in a tent in the bush. Fortunately, this was soon resolved when a local man offered to let Britney and Eliza live in a couple of unused rooms in his home. Soon Julie was also hanging out at the house and the trio was smoking away copious amounts of cannabis. They were also taking harder drugs, whenever they could get their hands on them.

And so, to the morning of June 18, 2006, and the murder that would catapult the small down of Collie onto the front page of every newspaper in Australia. Britney, Julie, and Eliza had hosted a party the previous evening, taking advantage of their landlord's absence. During the party, the girls had all smoked cannabis and taken the methamphetamine, 'Ice.' Eventually, after the festivities petered out at around 4 a.m., they had passed out, Eliza in one room, Britney and Julie in another. Then, on Sunday morning, Britney and Julie had woken up and started talking. Somehow, during the course of that conversation, they had decided to kill Eliza. "We did it because we felt like it," Britney later confessed. "It's hard to explain."

Having decided to commit murder, the girls changed into old clothes and started rooting around the house for the tools they'd need. A length of speaker wire would serve their purposes for strangulation, and they also rustled up a cloth and some household chemicals. This, they believed, could be used to render their victim unconscious. Eliza entered the room without any inkling of what was about to happen. She was immediately confronted by Julie, who clamped a chemical-soaked cloth over her mouth. Then Britney looped the speaker wire around her throat and pulled it tight.

Eliza fought hard for her life, but she was outnumbered and outmuscled. Eventually, her struggles subsided, and she went limp.

Brittney lowered her to the floor and Julie checked for a pulse. There was none. The juvenile killers then dragged their victim down to the dirt-floor cellar. There, they dug a two-foot-deep trench and buried her.

Later that afternoon, the police in Collie received a call from an apparently distressed Britney who reported that her friend, Eliza, was missing. A search was launched, with Britney among the civilian volunteers. Julie, meanwhile, had departed for Perth. She would remain there for the next three days before walking into a police station and confessing her part in the murder. At that very moment, Britney was doing the same, confessing to the police in Collie that she'd murdered her friend. These synchronized confessions had not been preplanned. It was just another odd twist in a bizarre case.

The most maddening thing about the murder was the total lack of a motive. Eliza had done nothing at all to antagonize her friends, she was just collateral damage in their quest to know how it felt to kill someone. "It just felt right," Brittney explained to detectives. "Or, at least, it didn't feel wrong." That was an incredibly paltry reason for destroying a young life.

Brittney and Julia went on trial for murder in May 2007. Found guilty on all charges, they were sentenced to life in prison, with parole eligibility in 15 years. Neither girl has ever expressed regret for the killing although Britney later claimed that she "feels sorry" for Eliza's family. Given the callous nature of her actions, it is difficult to take her declaration of remorse seriously.

Jeffrey Weise

On Jeffrey Weise's MSN page, he described himself as "16 years of accumulated rage suppressed by nothing more than brief glimpses of hope, which have all but faded to black." At school, he was a loner, teased for his towering height and his habit of wearing eyeliner, dressing all in black, and donning a long black trench coat, whatever the weather. He also admired Adolf Hitler and referred to himself as a 'Native Nazi.' If all of this leads you to the belief that Jeff Weise was a messed-up kid, you would not be mistaken.

Born in Minneapolis, Minnesota, in 1988, Jeff Weise was the only child of an unmarried couple, 17-year-old Joanne Weise and 21-year-old Daryl Lussier Jr. Both of his parents were members of the Ojibwe Native American tribe and lived on the Red Lake reservation, an unincorporated section of Beltrami County, Minnesota.

However, there would be no happy family to welcome the child into the world. His parents split before he was even born. Jeff would spend the first three months with his birth mother, before her parents forced her to give him up. He then passed into the custody of his father and would spend the first three years of his life living on the reservation. Then, in June 1991, Joanne showed up to reclaim her son, a move that would have disastrous consequences for Jeff. His mother was by now drinking heavily and would become physically and verbally abusive when she was drunk. As if that were not bad enough, she was dating a man who hated the boy and treated him badly. This mistreatment got even worse after the couple married.

And that was only the start of young Jeff's problems. In 1997, when he was eight, his biological father shot and killed himself during a standoff with the Red Lake Police Department. Two years later, in March 1999, his mother was involved in a serious auto accident, suffering brain damage as a result. Then her husband divorced her, taking Jeff's two stepsiblings but leaving Jeff behind. Since Joanne was no longer able to care for him, he ended up back on the Red Lake reservation, in the custody of his paternal grandfather, Daryl "Dash" Lussier Sr. Joanne would later regain her speech and some of her mental facilities, but Jeff chose to remain with his grandfather rather than return to his mother's dubious care.

As can be expected with such a chaotic childhood, Jeff attended numerous schools growing up. By the time he enrolled at Red Lake Senior High in 2003, he had already been a student at five different education facilities. One thing remained consistent though. Jeff Weise was trouble, prone to petulant outbursts, disruptive behavior, and frequent truancy. He also had learning disabilities and was enrolled for a time in a special education program. By now a hulking six-footer, he was nonetheless a target for bullies. That would not change at Red Lake High.

But at least Jeff had one thing going for him – a stable home life. His grandfather, Daryl Sr., was a police officer and the two of them got on well. Jeff also had a good relationship with Darryl's girlfriend, Michele Sigana, herself an officer with the Red Lake Police Department. All in all, things were looking up. For the first time in his life, Jeff had some stability.

In the mind of Jeff Weise, though, things were far from stable. The boy seems to have been inexplicably drawn to the dark side, to feelings of loneliness and despair. He expressed these in a notebook that he carried with him everywhere and also in online posts. Here, he painted a bleak picture of life in Red Lake, describing it as a place where "people choose alcohol over friendship" and where women "neglect their own flesh and blood for relationships with men." These posts were characterized by expressions of frustration and powerlessness. Death was a frequent theme. "I can't escape the grave I'm continually digging for myself," Weise typed in May 2004. Just a few days later, he slashed his wrists with a box opener.

The wound was not deep enough to cause death, but Jeff would make a second attempt – in June of 2004 – resulting in him being hospitalized, sent for counseling, and prescribed Prozac. The medication had little effect on his feelings of despair, though, and a doctor later upped the dosage, also to little avail. By March 2005, the boy was again contemplating suicide, writing in his notebook that he had been "driven to a darker path than most choose to take." That path would soon lead him to a third act of self-harm. Only, he'd do it right this time. And he would not make the journey to the afterlife alone.

All was quiet in the Lussier household on the afternoon of March 21, 2005. In the master bedroom, Daryl Lussier Sr. was asleep, resting up before his night shift; down in the basement, Daryl's girlfriend, Michelle, was doing the laundry; and up in his bedroom, 16-year-old Jeff Weise was lying on his bed, contemplating his plans for that afternoon. Jeff was currently on suspension from West Lake High and had not attended classes there for five weeks. Today he planned to return. Rising from his bed, he walked across to his closet. There, he started rooting around in a drawer, eventually retrieving a Ruger MK II .22 caliber pistol, that he'd been hiding for nearly a year. He removed the magazine, slotted it back in, and then cocked the weapon. That done, he set off in the direction of his grandfather's bedroom.

Daryl was fast asleep when his grandson entered. That suited the boy's purposes perfectly. He did not want his grandfather to know what was coming. Walking up to the sleeping form, he leveled the pistol. Then he started firing, emptying the magazine. The medical examiner would later retrieve twelve bullets from Daryl Lussier's head and chest.

With his grandfather dead, Jeff quickly commandeered his two police-issue weapons, a .40 caliber Glock pistol and a Remington 12-gauge pump-action shotgun. He also snapped on Daryl's gunbelt and bullet-proof vest. Then he headed towards the basement, catching Michelle as she was climbing the stairs, carrying a basket of laundry. The sound of the washing machine had drowned out the gunfire from upstairs. Michelle was oblivious until she saw Jeff standing in front of her with the gun raised. Two bullets from the Glock ended her life.

At around 2:45 that afternoon, a police cruiser pulled into the parking lot at Red Lake Senior High School. Only it wasn't a police officer at the wheel, it was Jeff Weise, driving his grandfather's vehicle. Getting out of the car, Weise walked confidently towards the main entrance, the Glock holstered, the Remington held loosely in his hand. Two unarmed security guards manned the entrance. One of them saw Weise coming and fled. The other, Derrick Brun, tried to reason with the boy and was shot dead. Weise then headed for a sophomore English class, where he opened fire, killing three students and a teacher, wounding three others. It might have been even worse had 16-year-old Jeffrey May not tackled Weise. May was one of those shot, suffering serious injuries to his neck and jaw. He would live, however. Others were not so lucky.

Leaving the classroom, Weise walked back towards the main entrance, encountering a group of students on route and opening up on them, killing two and wounding two more. By now, police officers had responded to the scene and some of them opened fire on Weise, sparking a fierce four-minute gun battle. During that skirmish, Weise was hit in the abdomen and right arm and retreated to an empty classroom. With police officers closing in on him, he positioned the shotgun barrel under his chin and pulled the trigger.

Ten people had been killed that day. Back at the Lussier residence, Daryl "Dash" Lussier and Michelle Sigana were yet to be discovered. In the blood-spattered halls of Red Lake High, the brave security guard, Derrick Brun, was dead. So too was English teacher, Neva Wynkoop-Rogers. And there were six student casualties – Dewayne Lewis, Chase Lussier, Chanelle Rosebear, and Thurlene Stillday were all 15 years old when they died. Alicia White was just 14.

Finally, there was the shooter himself, sitting on the floor in a vacant classroom with his brain matter splattered across the wall behind him. Jeffrey Weise's desperately unhappy life had brought him to this place. It would torment him no further.

Tronneal Mangum

He was just 14 years old and already a six-footer. He was also a bully, who enjoyed harassing his seventh-grade classmates at Conniston Middle School in West Palm Beach, Florida. One of his favorite targets was 14-year-old John Pierre Kamel, a boy of Egyptian descent who had a prosthetic leg due to a birth defect. Once, John Pierre and Tronneal Mangum had been friends. Now Troneal seemed to prefer teasing him and roughing him up. It was all typical schoolhouse roughhousing and John Pierre took most of it in his stride. But then there was the issue of the watch. That was when things escalated.

The watch in question was just an ordinary timepiece, a simple Adidas digital that John's mother had given him. Since the boy's parents were separated and he seldom saw his mom, the watch had a special significance for John. He proudly brought it to school and showed it around. That was when Tronneal Mangum showed up and asked to see the watch. John was happy to let him look at it but less keen when Troneal asked if he could put it on, to see how it looked on his wrist. Still, how was he going to refuse? Troneal towered over him and didn't usually take no for an answer. And so, John handed the watch over and Tronneal placed it on his wrist, gave it an admiring glance, and then walked away.

Over the days that followed, John asked Tronneal repeatedly to return his watch. When that failed, he took to begging, then to rounding up a group of classmates and getting them to confront the bully. Tronneal simply laughed them off and challenged them to take the watch off him. "This is mine now," he insisted. Eventually, the increasingly desperate John confided in his 19-year-old cousin, Tony Attalla, and asked him to speak to Troneal. Tony said that he would and arranged to meet John at the school on Monday morning, January 27, 1997. Unfortunately, he overslept. His laxity would have tragic consequences.

At around 8:40 a.m. on that Monday morning, with students streaming towards classes at Conniston Middle School, John Pierre spotted his nemesis standing on the sidewalk. Frustrated by his cousin's no-show, he decided to approach Troneal one last time, to make an appeal to his better nature. The boys had once been friends, after all. Perhaps he could persuade Troneal to do the right thing and give his watch back.

We don't know what was said between John Pierre and Troneal that morning. A short while after they exchanged greetings, three gunshots rang out and John Pierre Kamel collapsed to the ground. Then, as screaming students ran for cover, Troneal Mangum made a dash towards some bushes and then, after stopping there for a brief moment, walked calmly back towards the school, entered the building, and headed for his first class of the day. By now, teachers had already called 911 and police cruisers were racing towards the scene. The first officer was there in just minutes. He found John Pierre bleeding from a chest wound and barely conscious. The boy spoke just one word before blacking out: "Troneal." By the time an ambulance arrived, John Pierre Kamel was dead.

Finding the killer was easy. Several students had seen Troneal Mangum fire the fatal shots and had seen him make a run for the nearby bushes. Searching the area, officers quickly recovered the murder weapon, a .38 Special revolver. The cops then entered the school and headed for Mangum's classroom. As they entered, the boy immediately stood, threw up his hands, and said: "I give up! It was an argument."

Tronneal Mangum was charged with first-degree murder and went on trial in late 1997. He was tried as an adult and although his age meant that the death penalty was off the table, the 14-year-old still faced the very real prospect of spending the rest of his days behind bars. With a rock-solid case against him – one that included eyewitnesses, the murder weapon, and a confession – the defense had to come up with something in mitigation. Their strategy was two-pronged. First, they claimed that Mangum was mentally disabled, having suffered brain damage in a car accident some years earlier. Then they cited self-defense, saying that Mangum had been living in fear that he would be physically harmed by John Pierre Kamel and his friends. He had brought the gun to school for protection.

This last assertion was particularly far-fetched. Just days earlier, Mangum had laughed off attempts by a group of boys who had demanded the return of the watch. Those were hardly the actions of someone who felt intimidated. And even if Mangum had been living in fear, there was an easy way to resolve the issue, one that did not require a lethal response. All he had to do was to return the property he'd stolen.

The intimidation defense was invalid for another reason. John Pierre had been alone when he was shot. He had not had any friends to back him up. Was the jury really expected to believe that the six-foot-tall Mangum was so terrified of his five-foot-two rival that he drew a gun and shot him? No, it seemed pretty clear to everyone in the courtroom that Mangum had not acted in self-defense. In fact, there was strong evidence to suggest the contrary, that he had come to school that day intending to murder John Pierre Kamel. Another Conniston student testified that Mangum had shown him the gun on the school bus that morning and had said that he was going to "shoot John." The boy had not believed him and had not thought that the gun was real. His testimony was nonetheless crucial, since it proved premeditation.

On January 16, 1998, the jury deliberated for several hours before returning with its verdict. Troneal Mangum was guilty of premeditated murder. He was sentenced to life in prison without parole, the youngest defendant ever to receive that sentence in the state of Florida.

One mystery remained unresolved, though. Where had Troneal Mangum gotten the gun? It is a question that has never been resolved, despite the best efforts of the police and the ATF. All that we know is that the weapon had been stolen from the registered owner's car several years earlier. How it got from there into the hands of a 14-year-old remains unknown. Whoever gave it to the juvenile gunman is not only responsible for John Pierre Kamel's death, he is responsible for destroying Troneal Mangum's life too.

Bernadette Protti

High school can be a stressful time in the life of a teenager, a time when there is pressure to get good grades, to stay out of trouble, and, above all, to fit in. Nobody wants to be 'that kid,' the outsider, the outcast. Take Bernadette Protti for example. Back in 1984, Bernadette was a 15-year-old freshman, attending Miramonte High School in Orinda, an affluent city in Contra Costa County, California. Pretty and at least somewhat popular, Bernadette was never in danger of being cast adrift from the school's 'in crowd.' But Bernadette had ambitions that went beyond just fitting in. She wanted a spot on the school's yearbook committee. Even more than that, she wanted to be a cheerleader. Unfortunately, she'd be turned down on both counts. It was a twin rejection that left her bitter and angry.

Also attending Miramonte High that year was 15-year-old Kirsten Costas. The quintessential high school deb, Kirsten was from a wealthy family and was one of the most popular girls in school. She was also in Bernadette's inner circle and considered her a friend. What Kirsten didn't know was that Bernadette had begun to fixate on her, to blame her for all of the problems in her life. After all, Kirsten had a place on the yearbook committee. She was on the cheerleading squad. Those were spots that Bernadette believed should have been hers. She resented Kirsten for taking them from her. No one had any idea how deep that resentment ran.

On the afternoon of June 23, 1984, Kirsten's mom got a call from a girl who identified herself as Bernadette. She said that she was phoning on behalf of the Bob-o-Links, a sort of sorority group at Miramonte High. Kirsten had just joined the group and Bernadette wanted to invite her to an initiation dinner that night. The dinner was at eight and Bernadette said that she would pick Kirsten up herself. Since Kirsten wasn't home at the time, her mom promised to pass the message on.

And Bernadette was punctual, even if the dinner invitation turned out to be a ruse. Rather than driving to a restaurant, she stopped on a dark street and told Kirsten that she wanted to talk. She then started accusing her friend of being out to get her and of stealing her places on the cheerleading squad and yearbook committee. Kirsten was taken aback by these accusations. She assured Bernadette that she was wrong, that the selection process had been fair and open. She even offered to put in a good word for Bernadette with the cheerleading coach.

But Bernadette was beyond listening to reason. She was becoming increasingly animated, so angry in fact that Kirsten began to fear for her safety. Eventually, she jumped out of the car and ran to the nearest house. There she banged on the door, rousing Alex Arnold.

He was suddenly faced with a frantic teenager who told him that her friend was "acting weird." She asked if she could use the phone to call her parents. Arnold, of course, said yes. After Kirsten made her call and got no reply, he offered to drive her home.

The Costas residence was only a short distance away. Before long, Alex Arnold and his passenger were pulling up outside. Noticing that the house was in darkness, Kirsten commented that her parents were probably out. Arnold told her that he'd wait at the curb until she was safely inside. Kirsten thanked him and got out of the vehicle. She started walking across the lawn. Then, out of nowhere, a figure came sprinting out of the dark and tackled her to the ground.

The struggle lasted no more than a few seconds. Sitting in his car, Alex Arnold saw several blows struck before the attacker ran off. He immediately set off in pursuit but stopped halfway down the block when he realized that he should probably check on Kirsten. By the time he got back, one of the Costas' neighbors had emerged and was attending to the stricken girl. It was then that Arnold saw the blood and realized what he had just witnessed. He'd thought that it was a fistfight. Now he saw that Kirsten had been brutally stabbed.

Kirsten Costas was rushed to a nearby hospital and taken immediately into surgery. But it was already too late. Just five knife wounds had been inflected but they ran deep and had pierced vital organs and blood vessels. The weapon used was later determined to have at least an 18-inch blade. Most probably, it was a kitchen knife. Kirsten never stood a chance. She died on the operating table.

In the aftermath of the tragedy, a pall of fear descended on the city of Orinda. People stayed home at night and doors and windows were securely locked. There were fears that a psychopath was stalking the streets. The police, meanwhile, were conducting their inquiries, which included questioning the dead girl's friends. Since Bernadette had picked Kirsten up that night, she came in for particular scrutiny but held up well under interrogation. She even passed a lie detector test. Bernadette admitted to the police that she had invented the story of the Bob-o-Links dinner. But she denied that she had done so for any sinister purpose. She had only wanted to get Kirsten alone so that she could talk to her about their failing friendship. Kirsten, however, had become angry when she learned that the dinner invitation was a lie. She had jumped out of the car and run off into the night. That was the last time that Bernadette had seen her alive.

Bernadette's story about her last, fateful meeting with her friend would stand up to police scrutiny for nearly six months. Indeed, it would have held up even longer. It might even have allowed a killer to get away with murder. But then Bernadette started to feel the prickling of conscience. Eventually, she could keep her secret no longer and confessed to the murder in a letter she wrote to her mother and left on the kitchen counter before going to school on the morning of December 10, 1984. By the end of the day, she would be in custody.

Bernadette Protti was now in a precarious position. Should the state decide to try her as an adult, she was looking at the possibility of life in prison without parole. Fortunately for Bernadette, her case would fall under the jurisdiction of the juvenile authorities. Found guilty of second-degree murder, she was sentenced to a maximum of nine years in prison. She would serve just seven of those years before her release in June 1992. Thereafter, she promptly left California and changed her name. Her current whereabouts are unknown, although she is rumored to be married and living in Oregon.

Peter Barratt & James Bradley

In February of 1993, a particularly shocking story came to dominate the world's media. A two-year-old had been abducted from a shopping mall in Bootle, Liverpool, taken to an embankment near rail lines, and beaten to death, his mutilated body left beside the tracks. That alone would have marked this as a quite horrific case but what made this murder particularly harrowing was the identity of the killers. They were Robert Thompson and Jon Venables, two ten-year-olds who had killed the toddler for no reason other than their own gratification.

Even today, over two decades later, the details of James Bulger's murder still have the capacity to shock. It seems so depraved, so senseless, so uniquely evil. It may therefore surprise you to learn that it is not unique, that another, startlingly similar, child murder occurred a mere thirty miles from where James' body was found. It happened over 100 years earlier in April 1861.

Two-year-old George Burgess was a lovely little boy. Blond-haired, lively, and talkative, he was much loved in the working-class neighborhood of Higher Hillgate, in Stockport, Lancashire, where he lived. George was the son of Ralph Burgess who worked as a cotton weaver, and Hannah Burgess, who also worked in the town's textile industry. Ralph and Hannah had two other sons – William, one, and Ralph, three months old. But while the younger boys lived with their parents, George had been placed in the permanent care of Sarah Ann Warren, a nurse who lived nearby. We don't know the reason for this unusual arrangement, but we do know that Ralph visited his son regularly. Usually, he'd stop off on his way home from work to spend a few minutes with the boy.

On the evening of Thursday, April 11, 1861, Ralph Burgess followed his regular routine of visiting George. This visit, however, would be anything but regular. Ralph arrived to find a frantic Sarah Ann Warren. George was missing. She'd last seen him playing with another toddler in a field across from her house. Now, he was nowhere to be found.

Ralph Burgess immediately launched a search for his son. He even engaged the town crier, at considerable cost, to walk the streets, informing residents to be on the lookout for the little boy. When all of these efforts proved fruitless, he went to the police and reported George missing. Several constables were then assigned, some focusing on the town while others fanned out to search the adjacent fields, streams, and reservoirs. They feared that George had wandered off and gotten lost or had met with an accident.

Unfortunately, these initial efforts brought no results. George's father would spend the entire night looking for him while his mother and guardian slept not wink while worrying about his whereabouts and wellbeing. When the mystery of the little boy's disappearance was finally resolved, at around noon the next day, it was in tragic circumstances. George was found by a farm laborer, his naked corpse floating face down in a shallow brook. The initial impression was accidental drowning but that was soon dismissed when the police saw the injuries to his body. The child was covered in cuts and abrasions and had a number of dark stripes crisscrossing his back. It appeared as though someone had taken a whip to him.

The coroner's report would later reveal the horrific extent of George's injuries. His back and buttocks had been lashed bloody, most probably with a rod of some kind. He had also suffered severe head trauma which the coroner thought had been inflicted with a log or a heavy stick. This would have left him concussed but he would still have been conscious when his killer forced his head underwater and held it there, causing him to drown. It was a truly horrific crime, inflicted on an entirely helpless victim.

The question was, who would have done such a thing to an innocent little boy? As the police started to question the residents of surrounding farms, they soon began to pick up on a couple of likely suspects. George had been seen in the company of two older boys that afternoon, who witnesses estimated to be around nine or ten years old. One witness, Mary Whitehead, said she had seen these boys with the toddler just before three o'clock. The little boy was crying and one of the older boys was dragging him along. She'd asked them where they were going and they had replied, "down Love Lane." She'd left it at that.

A short while later, Emma Williams and her teenaged son, Frank, had also spotted the ill-matched threesome. Emma had demanded to know where the older boys were taking the child, but they had run off without answering. Frank had noticed that one of the boys was carrying a stick which he used to hit the child. Again, nothing was done to intervene on George's behalf. (This has tragic echoes of the Bulger case.)

The police would eventually gather several eyewitness statements, including some that named the two boys involved. Peter Barratt and James Bradley were well-known juvenile thugs and delinquents. They had recently been ejected from the local church school for ripping up Bibles and for bullying younger children. Barratt and Bradley were, however, younger than the initial witnesses had estimated. As incredible as it seems, the murder suspects were just eight years old.

Peter Barratt was sweeping the floor in his father's barbershop when the police arrived to question him. Barratt senior seemed unconcerned by the accusations levied against his son saying only that he "couldn't have done it." He also had no hesitation in permitting the police to question the boy and happily continued to cut a customer's hair while the interrogation took place in a back room. Then he allowed the officers to take his son to James Bradley's house, again not bothering to accompany them. There, the two boys were brought face to face and soon confessed to the crime. "It were Peter that hit it with the stick," Bradley asserted.

"Well, thou hit it as well as me," Barratt responded angrily. They were at a loss to explain, however, why they had attacked the two-year-old in the first place.

Peter Barratt and James Bradley were brought before an inquest at the White House Tavern in Stockport on Tuesday, April 16. The purpose of the inquiry was to determine whether there was sufficient evidence to bring charges. The mood in the crowded room was ugly. Just the previous day, thousands had lined the route as George Burgess' tiny coffin was taken by carriage to its final resting place at Christ Church cemetery. But for a sizeable police presence, things inside the tavern might have gotten out of hand.

In the end, though, the crowd was satisfied with the jury's decision. The law of the land was clear. A child seven years or younger could not be charged with willful murder. A child of eight could be charged if there was evidence that showed his or her understanding of right and wrong. In this case, the jury decided that there was enough to support a murder charge. Barratt and Bradley were therefore indicted and taken into custody to await trial.

The trial of Peter Barratt and James Bradley began at the Chester Summer Assizes on August 8, 1861. During the intervening four months, relations between the co-accused had soured. They had begun to quarrel and, on one occasion, Barratt had attacked his smaller companion with a belt buckle. Now, though, they were united in facing a very serious charge. For the next nine hours, the court would hear evidence, much of it the same as had been presented at the inquest, all of it damning. Since the question of guilt had never been denied, this was the epitome of an open and shut case.

But there was one key difference. Whereas the inquest jury had been happy to return a murder indictment, the trial judge had other ideas. He made his views clear in his instructions to the jury, describing the decision to bring willful murder charges against defendants so young as "stretching the spirit of the law." That left the jury with very little wiggle room, and they returned within 15 minutes to declare that the accused were innocent of murder but guilty of manslaughter. The judge then sentenced them to the Reformatory at Bradwall for a period of five years. The boys, who had been laughing and joking up to that point, started crying after the sentence was read.

James Bradley would serve four-and-a-half years of his five-year sentence at Bradwell, before gaining his freedom in 1866. His fate, after his release, is unknown. Peter Barratt's fate is even less certain. He did not complete his sentence at the liberal Bradwell but was later transferred to the far stricter Warwickshire Weston Colony. That seems to suggest that he had behavioral issues. Many of the Warwickshire inmates were 'transported' to Australia or Canada after their sentences were completed and that may well have happened to Barratt. Certainly, he does not appear on any subsequent Cheshire or Warwickshire census records.

Jaylen Fryberg

Jaylen Fryberg was a young man with a lot going for him. A freshman at Marysville-Pilchuck High in Marysville, Washington, Jaylen was a popular kid, with a sunny outlook on life. He had a large circle of friends and a steady girlfriend in 15-year-old Shilene George; he was a keen athlete, who represented his school at wrestling and football; he'd recently been announced as the freshman homecoming prince. But then, sometime in mid-2014, something changed. Jaylen became quieter, more withdrawn. His academic performance, never spectacular to begin with, slipped. His girlfriend broke up with him. She said that he'd become violent towards her.

No one could say what it was that brought about this dramatic change in Jaylen. Later, after the dust had settled, many would put it down to a fight that he had with another student. During the course of that altercation, his adversary had used a racial slur. Jaylen was a member of the Tulalip Native American tribe and proud of his heritage. The jibe cut deeply, even when friends told him to ignore it. And there were other consequences to the fight, too. Jaylen was suspended from school and cut from the football team. It was when he returned from suspension that his friends first noticed the change in him. Some of them even tried to talk to him about it but Jaylen insisted that everything was fine and so they let it be.

On October 24, 2014, Several of Jaylen's inner circle received a text from him, asking to meet up in the school cafeteria at 10:40 that morning. Some of them protested that they had classes at that time, but Jaylen urged them to skip out, saying that what he had to tell them was important. Intrigued by this, all of them eventually agreed. Included in the invited group were Jaylen's cousins, Andrew Fryberg and Nate Hatch, Andrew's girlfriend, Zoë Galasso, and two other girls, Gia Soriano and Shaylee Chuckulnaskit.

The group was already seated at a table, among around 150 other students in the cafeteria, when Jaylen entered at 10:39. Intriguingly, he did not sit with his friends but dropped into a seat at a nearby table. For a while, he sat there, furiously typing into his cellphone. Then he rose and walked across to where his friends were sitting. Nate flashed him a smile, but Jaylen didn't return it. Instead, he launched into a verbal tirade against his startled friends. Soon every other student in the room was looking up, trying to determine the source of the ruckus. That was when Jaylen Fryberg drew a gun and started firing.

The gunshots sounded incredibly loud inside the cafeteria. It sparked an immediate panic, with students screaming and stampeding for the exits. But they needn't have worried. The shooter wasn't interested in them. He had specific targets in mind, and they were all seated around this one table. Calmly and methodically, Fryberg picked his targets, took aim, and pulled off his shots. Eight bullets were fired in the matter of perhaps 30 seconds. Zoë Galasso was hit in the face. So too were Gia Soriano, Shaylee Chuckulnaskit, and Andrew Fryberg. Nate Hatch was also hit and so were two other boys seated at the table. Unable to flee, those wounded students were now at the shooter's mercy.

In many of the tragic school shootings that plague our society, there are tales of heroism, of some individual who steps into the breach at great personal risk and prevents further bloodshed. In this case, it was a first-year social studies teacher named Megan Silberberger.

The teacher had almost been trampled in the initial stampede but had forced her way past the panicked rush of kids to confront Fryberg. She made a grab for Fryberg's arm, but Fryberg shook her off. Had he decided to turn the gun on her, there would have been little that Ms. Silberberger could have done about it. But Fryberg didn't do that. Instead, he raised the gun to his own head and pulled the trigger. As he collapsed to the floor, Megan Silberberger reached for her phone and punched in 911 with shaking hands. But for her intervention, Fryberg might well have finished the job on the students that he'd initially winged.

As it was, Fryberg had exacted a heavy toll. The first police officer was on the scene within minutes but was already too late. The shooter, Jaylen Fryberg, was dead. So too, was 14-year-old Zoë

Galasso. Gia Soriano, Shaylee Chuckulnaskit, Andrew Fryberg, and Nate Hatch were all seriously injured and were rushed to a nearby hospital. Hatch would survive his wounds, but the other three victims would all succumb to their injuries over the next week. Soriano and Chuckulnaskit were just 14 years old on the day that they died. Andrew Fryberg was 15. The two other students who had been hit had suffered only slight injuries. They were treated and discharged that same day.

In the aftermath of the shooting, there would be many questions asked, few of which would garner satisfactory answers. The first, and perhaps most important, was why? Why would a student who had been described by classmates and teachers as a "really nice kid," suddenly turn into a homicidal maniac?

Many answers have been proffered – Fryberg's angry reaction to the racial slur directed at him; his breakup with his girlfriend; his axing from the football team. None of these make sense if we look at the victims he targeted. He must have borne some particular grudge against these individuals and the closest we get is his romantic overtures towards Zoë Galasso and her rejection of those advances. Zoë had been dating Fryberg's cousin, Andrew, and had told him that she cared for Andrew and was happy in the relationship. Was it perhaps that perceived slight that tipped Jaylen over the edge? Certainly, the first shots that he fired were aimed at Zoë and Andrew. Since Jaylen is not here to answer for his actions, we will never know for certain.

Aside from motive, the key evidentiary question for the police was the source of the murder weapon. It was a .40-caliber Beretta Px4

Storm handgun that belonged to Fryberg's father. It turned out that Raymond Lee Fryberg was barred from owning a gun due to a previous order of protection against him for domestic violence offenses. Fryberg had lied about this on the application form and had, in fact, acquired five firearms since the banning order. He was ultimately prosecuted for these offenses and sentenced to two years in prison.

One other mystery still needed to be resolved. What had Jaylen Fryberg been typing into his phone just before he launched his deadly attack? The answer to that is both startling and bizarre. He had typed up a group text message to the families of his victims, apologizing for what he was about to do. A second message went to his own family, laying out plans for his funeral.

David Brom

It started with a fight over music. David Brom had been raised in a strict Catholic home and his father, Bernard, took exception to the songs he was listening to, particularly one by the band Negativland called 'Christianity is Stupid.' Bernard Brom forbade his son from listening to the song and ordered him to remove the album from his house. A typically rebellious teenager, 16-year-old David refused, saying that he was old enough to make his own decisions. The argument quickly got heated and raged on until around 11:30 that Wednesday evening, February 17, 1988. Then Bernard went to bed, telling his son that they would resolve things in the morning. With a truce temporarily in place, the rest of the family soon drifted off to sleep. But not David. He was up in his room, angrily pacing the floor, fuming at the injustice of it all. Eventually, he decided what he must do and headed down to the basement. When he emerged a few minutes later, he was carrying an ax.

The following morning, February 18, David Brom showed up as usual at Lourdes High School, where he was a sophomore. But this was no ordinary day. For starters, he was driving his father's van, something he was usually not allowed to do. And he did not actually attend classes. As soon as the bell rang, to signal the start of the academic day, he drove off. He'd spend the rest of that day cruising the streets of his hometown, Rochester, Minnesota. During that time, he visited Kutzky Park, Kmart, and Godfather's Pizza. Then he made a stop at his house before heading for an ATM and withdrawing $250 from his father's bank account.

By this time, however, a worrying rumor had reached the ears of the authorities at Lourdes High School. During his brief visit to the school that morning, David Brom had confided in a female friend that he had murdered his parents. Since he was prone to making outrageous statements, the girl had not believed him. However, she had told another student and the story had spread like wildfire from there. Eventually, a teacher got to hear it and reported it to a school administrator. The administrator then contacted the Olmsted County Sheriff's department and asked if they would send a cruiser to the Brom residence to check on the family. The deputies arrived just before 6 p.m. They expected it to be a routine wellbeing check. It wasn't.

Bernard Brom and his wife, Paulette, were in their bedroom, savagely hacked to death, their blood spattered on walls and furnishings, pooled on the carpet, even sprayed across the ceiling. They weren't the only victims. Their 13-year-old daughter, Diane, had been killed and so had their son Ricky, just 11-years of age. The medical examiner would later count 56 wounds inflicted on the victims. The murder weapon, a bloodstained ax with a 28-inch handle, was found lying on the ground at the bottom of the basement stairs. Judging by the condition of the corpses, it was determined that the family had been killed within the last 12 hours, more than likely in the pre-dawn hours of February 18. That meant that the family had already been dead by the time David Brom arrived at school that Thursday morning.

But where was David? A massive manhunt was launched for the youth, one that roped in the public via local media. David Brom's face was soon staring out from television sets across the county. And it quickly paid dividends. Later that day, one of David's former teachers reported a sighting of him at a local mall. Officers responded but found no trace of the teen. They did, however, locate the van, found abandoned at nearby Methodist Hospital. Then there was another report, this one received at around 8:30 on Friday morning. Brom had been spotted by a member of the public, using a payphone at Rochester's main post office. Police officers immediately flooded into the area and took Brom into custody. He offered no resistance when the cuffs were snapped on him and was similarly subdued when he was arraigned at Olmsted County Court later that day. The indictment was for four counts of first-degree murder and there were already moves underway to try Brom as an adult.

But how had it come to this? How could such a bloody crime be attributed to a boy who was well-liked by his classmates and teachers, who had been raised in a strict but loving home, who did well at school, who had never been in trouble with the law? It turns out that David Brom had some serious mental health issues. He had been suffering from severe depression for years and had twice attempted suicide, the last time just months before the murders. It appeared that he had also been contemplating another way out of his predicament. Over the prior six months, he had spoken frequently about killing his parents. The friends who he had confided in had thought he was just blowing off steam.

As the matter headed for trial, there was the usual legal tussle over the status of the defendant. Initially, a judge had ruled that the Brom case would be heard in juvenile court, but the prosecution filed an appeal and the State Supreme Court eventually ruled in their favor. David Brom would face trial as an adult.

This left Brom's defense team in a difficult situation, with no other option but to plead their client 'not guilty by reason of insanity.' This is always a risk. It seldom succeeds in a murder trial and in this case the prosecution had a witness who would cast doubt on the issue of insanity – the student who Brom had confessed to on the day of the murders. Called as a prosecution witness, the girl's testimony was a chilling account of the slaughter.

"He said that he hit his dad with an ax and kept hitting him as he tried to get up," she told a hushed courtroom. According to the witness, Brom had told her that he'd gotten into an argument with his father the previous evening. This had ended at around 11:30 when his father had gone to bed. Brom, however, had been unable to sleep. He had remained awake until around 3 a.m. when he had decided to kill his father. He'd fetched the long-handled ax from the basement for that purpose. David had thought that one blow to the head would be enough to end his father's life, but he'd had to strike several times before his father eventually lay still. The struggle, however, had woken his mother, and so he had to kill her too. He'd then walked to his brother's room and hacked the 11-year-old to death as he slept. Finally, he'd gone looking for his sister, but her bed was empty. He'd found her in their parents' room, trying to revive their mother. A swing of the ax had ended her life. Brom had provided no motive for killing his siblings.

It was a damning indictment, backed up by the bloody palm print found on the handle of the ax. But Brom wasn't denying murder. His defense was that he'd been insane at the time of the killings. What would the jury make of that?

Unfortunately for Brom, his insanity defense never stood a chance. Minnesota relies on a strict interpretation of the M'Naghten Rules. That means Brom would only be judged legally insane if a mental illness or defect prevented him from determining right from wrong at the moment of the crime. Since that was clearly not the case, his plea was rejected.

David Brom was convicted of four counts of first-degree murder. He was sentenced to four life terms and is currently inmate No. 146854 at the Minnesota Correctional Facility in Stillwater.

Natsumi Tsuji

Natsumi Tsuji was a typical Japanese schoolgirl, a grade six student attending classes at an elementary school in Sasebo, a city in the Nagasaki Prefecture. Like most of her classmates, the 11-year-old was obedient, devoted to her studies, and looking forward to moving on to junior high in the next year. But in 2004, something happened to Natsumi. She discovered the internet and, more specifically, an animated horror clip called "The Red Room."

The Red Room was a somewhat crude, flash-based animation, in keeping with the technology of the day. But it was nonetheless creepy, in the way that only Japanese horror seems to achieve. The plot involves a boy telling his friend about a website called The Red Room. The other boy is only vaguely interested but when he goes home, he decides to check it out. However, he can't find the site via a search and soon loses interest. He continues surfing the web, visiting his favorite sites when suddenly a pop-up appears. It reads: "Do you like me?" The boy closes it and continues surfing but then the message re-appears. "Do you like me?" Annoyed, the boy shuts it down again. Almost immediately, a new pop-up opens, "Do you like The Red Room?" Then pop-ups start opening and closing at random, each one telling a snippet of a story involving a knife-wielding killer. Finally, the pop-ups start listing names. The boy sees his friend's name there, then his own. Scared now, he tries to call his friend, to ask him how to shut down the game. But his friend's phone rings without being answered. Then there is a knock at the door. He goes to answer it and is attacked by the mysterious killer and slashed to death.

As absurd as this storyline is, it had a big impact on Natsumi Tsuji. In fact, it began to take over her life. She became obsessed with The Red Room and started searching online for more information. That was how she came across a chatroom for fans of the story. She began lurking at first, then responding to posts and eventually starting threads of her own. Through these activities, she was introduced to Guro, an extreme form of manga and anime which focuses heavily on gore and mutilation. She also read the controversial novel, Battle Royale, and watched its film adaptation. The story, widely considered to be the inspiration for The Hunger Games, centers on a group of young students pitted against each other in a fight to the death. While exploring these dark themes, Natsumi met a like-minded soul from her school, a 12-year-old named Satomi Miratai. Drawn together by their mutual interests, the two quickly became friends.

By now, Natsumi's teachers had begun to notice a worrying change in her behavior. She had become increasingly aggressive and would respond to any insult, real or perceived, by threatening violence against the offender. Sometimes, she even carried through on these threats, punching, kicking, and choking her classmates. This behavior is hardly surprising when you consider the disturbing influences in Natsumi's life, influences which now included a Korean TV show called "Monday Mystery Theatre." The hour-long episodes usually featured storylines with bizarre and macabre content. One that made a particular impression on Natsumi was about a serial killer who slashed his victims to death with a box-cutter. Shortly after watching this episode, Natsumi threatened to do the same to a boy in her class. Although she was reprimanded for making the threat, no further action was taken.

And so to the event that would propel Natsumi Tsuji onto the front page of every newspaper in Japan. It started with a dispute between Natsumi and her best friend Satomi over a forum post. Satomi had commented that Natsumi was "heavy" i.e., overweight. Although this was untrue, the comment seemed to really get under Natsumi's skin. She demanded that Satomi "take it back," something that Satomi refused to do. Satomi then added insult to injury by calling Natsumi "a fraud" and "a goody-two-shoes." That, for Natsumi, was the ultimate insult. She would not allow herself to be disrespected in this way.

On the afternoon of Tuesday, June 1st, 2004, during the lunch break at Sasebo Elementary School, Natsumi asked Satomi to go with her to a storeroom on the school grounds. Perhaps surprisingly, given the strained relations between the two, Satomi agreed. She even sat down in a chair when Natsumi instructed her to do so. She then listened calmly as her friend told her that she was about to die. Perhaps she thought this was a re-enactment of one of the internet memes they were both so fond of. If that was what she believed, she was horribly mistaken.

According to Natsumi's later retelling of events, Satomi sat
passively as Natsumi removed her glasses. Natsumi then asked if
she wanted a blindfold. Satomi said that she did not, so Natsumi
placed her left hand over her friend's eyes instead. With her right,
she withdrew a box cutter from her pocket and extended its razor-
sharp blade. In a flash, she drew it across Satomi's throat, cutting
deep, severing every vein and artery on its path.

Satomi slumped immediately to the floor, hands flying to the
wound in a vain attempt to stem the flow of blood. There was
never a chance that she would survive the horrendous wound.
Still, Natsumi wasn't taking any chances. As the flow of blood
weakened, as Satomi's convulsions ceased and she lapsed into
unconsciousness, Natsumi applied the box-cutter again, this time
using it to slash through her friend's wrists. She then walked
calmly back to class in her blood-soaked school uniform and
informed a teacher, "I have done something bad."

By the time police and paramedics arrived on the scene, Satomi
Miratai was already dead. Natsumi was taken into custody and
would spend the night in a police cell, crying and repeating over
and over, "I'm sorry, I'm sorry." During initial interviews, she
refused to discuss her motive for the murder although she later
admitted that it was over an online squabble during which Satomi
had called her "fat" and a "goody-goody."

Japanese law prohibited Natsumi Tsuji from being tried for
murder or even being publicly named. Throughout the extensive

media coverage of the case, she was referred to only as 'Girl A.' Then an official inadvertently let her name slip during a TV broadcast and it became public knowledge. Media outlets were then warned against printing Tsuji's photograph although the ban would have little impact since numerous websites had already published pictures purporting to be of the juvenile killer. In the most common iteration, Natsumi is pictured wearing a University of Nevada sweatshirt, leading to her being nicknamed "Nevada-tan" in the media and in popular culture. Over time, Nevada-tan would develop a cult-like status online, with various amines showing her in a bloody Nevada shirt, holding a box-cutter dripping with blood.

But that lay in the future. For now, the Japanese legal system had to decide what to do about Natsumi Tsuji. The age of criminal responsibility had recently been lowered in Japan, in the wake of the 1997 Kobe child murders, committed by 14-year-old Shinichirou Azuma. But at just 11 years of age, Tsuji was still well below the age limit.

On September 15, 2004, a Family Court ruled that Tsuji should be incarcerated at the Tochigi Juvenile Institute for two years. Later, an additional two years was added to the term. In the interim, it had been announced that Tsuji had been diagnosed with Asperger syndrome, a form of autism.

Natsumi Tsuji was released in 2008. Her current whereabouts are not known.

Alex Crain

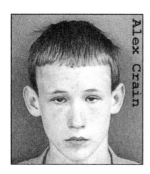

From the outside, they looked like a perfectly normal family. Forty-year-old Thomas Crain ran a successful screening and aluminum siding company from his home at Golden Gate Estates, in Naples, Florida. His wife Kelly, 39, was his partner in the business. The couple had one child, a 14-year-old son named Alex, who was a freshman at Palmetto Ridge High. Alex was an average kid who had typical teenage issues but nothing to cause undue alarm to his parents. A couple of years earlier, he'd been suspended from school for throwing a rock at another kid. Other than that, there had been no major issues. All in all, the Crains lived an ordinary, middle-class life.

But on the evening of December 9, 2010, that picture of suburban bliss would be shattered in the most brutal way possible. At around 8:30 that night, a hysterical Alex placed a 911 call and told a stunned Collier County dispatcher, "I was sleeping and the next thing I know I had a gun in my hand and my parents were on the ground." He then spent sixteen minutes on the line, talking to the dispatcher while police and paramedics raced towards his location. During that time, he tearfully assured the dispatcher that he had not argued with his parents, that he loved them, and that he was not on any medication. He also begged her to "make the emergency services hurry up" because his parents were not going to make it. Finally, when the police arrived, he exited the residence and walked down the driveway with his hands up, like some desperado surrendering to the lawmen that had been pursuing him.

Thomas was quickly subdued, cuffed, and placed into the back of a patrol car. Only then did officers enter the house to discover the bloodbath within. Thomas Crain lay on the floor of the master bedroom, shot in the back, the bullet entering just below the right shoulder. His wife, Kelly, was half in and half out of the shower in the master bathroom. She had been shot in the head. The murder weapon, a .30-caliber rifle, lay discarded on the bathroom floor.

There was never any doubt as to who had killed the Crains. Fourteen-year-old Alex made no pretense at innocence. At that very moment, he was sitting in the back of the police car, crying, and occasionally shouting out, "I'm sorry! I didn't mean to hurt them!" He would later be observed on the vehicle's video system, bashing his head against the side window while shouting, "I shouldn't have done it. What the f**k is wrong with me? I shot my own parents for no f**king reason."

Despite his declarations of remorse, Alex Crain was charged with two counts of murder and taken to the Collier County Juvenile

Detention Facility where he would undergo three weeks of evaluation, while the State decided whether to try him as a juvenile or as an adult. This was not a decision to be taken lightly, since it would have major implications for the young man. A juvenile conviction would see him serve less than seven years and be eligible for mandatory release by the age of 21. If tried and convicted in an adult court, he could be facing life in prison.

Alex Crain's period of evaluation would ultimately last a lot longer than the proposed three weeks. He would spend three months under observation, during which time he was subjected to a battery of psychiatric tests. What the doctors really wanted to know was why he'd done it. Had he been beaten? Sexually abused? Unfairly treated? Alex assured them that none of these was true, that he loved his parents and deeply regretted harming them. His only explanation was the one he'd given to the 911 dispatcher on the night of the murders, that he had found himself in his parents' bedroom holding the gun, his parents lying dead at his feet.

Friends, family, and teachers were unable to add to that. They all reported an ordinary family with no forewarning of the horrible tragedy to come. That, as it turned out, was not entirely true. As the matter headed towards trial, there were clues, subtle clues admittedly, that all was not well with Alex.

The first of these was a story that started doing the rounds about a conversation Alex had with a classmate, about a month before the murders. The boy had been teasing him about going everywhere with his mother and Alex had responded that he was just winning her trust so that she wouldn't be expecting it when he killed her.

The classmate later denied that Alex had ever made these comments, although he did admit teasing him about being a "mommy's boy."

Then there was something that a neighbor reported to the police during their inquiries, an incident that had also happened about a month before the murders. The woman had heard gunshots coming from the Crain residence, while Alex was home alone. She had later reported this to the boy's parents, but Alex had denied firing the rifle. According to him, he'd been letting off firecrackers. The neighbor, though, was adamant that she'd heard gunshots. She later heard the same sound on the night that Thomas and Kelly were killed. Had Alex been getting in some target practice?

Another interesting revelation came from one of Alex's cousins. About a year before the shootings, Alex had told him that he'd called 911 and reported his father for abuse after Thomas had slapped him for taking a soda from the fridge without permission. It is uncertain whether this incident ever happened or if the call was, in fact, made. However, it does point to feelings of animosity that Alex may have harbored towards his father.

And then there was something that happened on the day before the shooting, something that suggests premeditation and makes a lie of Alex Crain's version of events. Alex had told a female classmate that this was to be his last day at school. Asked why, he'd said that his parents' house was being foreclosed and that they would be leaving the area. This was untrue and smacks of a story concocted on the spot. What Alex was really hinting at was the murder of his parents.

But what of motive? We have already seen that there was some difficulty between father and son and that Alex was quite attached to his mother. Does that get us any closer to why he gunned them down? The answer may lie in a piece of evidence uncovered by the police during the initial search of the Crain residence. Under Alex's mattress, officers found a handwritten note which said: "Why am I always second best?" In the same location, they found two pairs of thong panties.

So what does this tell us? Who was it that Alex Crain felt he was second best to? Since he had no siblings, we can only assume that he was referring to his relationship with his parents. We know that he was close to his mother and was even teased about this by a classmate. Was he jealous of his mother's closeness with his father? Did he feel excluded from the relationship that his parents had with each other? Is that what drove him to pick up a gun and shoot them both down? Unless Alex Crain decides to open up about these things, we will never know for sure.

In March 2011, Assistant State Attorney Richard Montecalvo made the announcement that Alex Crain and his defense team had been dreading. Alex would be tried as an adult, the only consolation being that the charges had been reduced from murder to manslaughter. That still meant that Crain faced the prospect of 60 years in prison.

The defense responded to this by asking to have Crain evaluated by its own psychiatrist, a move that suggested they were considering an insanity defense. Whether that was true or not, it put pressure on the prosecutor, bringing him to the negotiating table to work out a plea bargain. The deal that was ultimately struck saw Crain enter an Alford plea (no contest) to two counts of manslaughter and accept a term of 20 years behind bars.

Alex Crain is currently serving his time at the Desoto Correctional Institution in Arcadia, Florida. He will be eligible for parole in October 2029, when he will be 31 years old.

Robert & Jeffrey Dingham

Depending on who you ask, Vance and Eve Dingham were either devoted parents or they were child abusers who subjected their sons to frequent physical and verbal mistreatment. Depending on who you ask, Robert and Jeffrey Dingham were either a couple of put-upon kids desperate to escape a dysfunctional home, or they were a pair of spoilt brats who had grown tired of living by their parents' (quite reasonable) rules. Either way, it didn't have to end this way. It didn't have to end in brutal, bloody murder.

The Dinghams, Vance and Eve and their two teenaged sons, lived in Rochester, New Hampshire. Vance was an electrician; Eve worked as a customer service representative. The boys – Robert, aged 17, and 14-year-old Jeffrey – were in high school and junior high respectively. Vance and Eve were, by all accounts, strict parents. According to Jeffrey's later testimony, his father would beat him and his brother if they brought home bad grades. His mother was always shouting, he said, flying off the handle at the slightest provocation. The boys also had a strict curfew in place and there'd be hell to pay if they ever broke it. The situation left them both desperately unhappy.

And so, the brothers decided to do something about it, something desperate. It was Robert who first suggested the idea, sometime in late 1995. "Why don't we just kill them?" he asked. It took only a moment of reflection before Jeffrey responded that he was in.

Over the next three months, the brothers considered various methods of carrying out the murders, including poisoning and drowning in the bathtub. But they finally settled on the simplest method of all – shooting. Their father owned a .22-caliber pistol that would do the job just fine. With that decided, they set a date. They would kill their parents on Friday, February 9, 1996.

The siblings' plan was simple. They'd steal the key to their father's gun safe, liberate the .22, and then lie in wait until their parents got home. On Fridays, it was usually Vance who walked through the door first, and thus it was on this day. Vance entered the house at around 4:30 p.m. and found himself confronted by his 14-year-old son, holding the pistol. He started to say something, but his words were cut short when Jeffrey pulled the trigger and the gun barked. Vance instantly clutched at his chest. "I can't believe my own son did this," he said as blood welled between his fingers. It was at that point that Robert took the gun from his younger brother.

"Oh yeah?" he growled. "How about another one?" Then he fired, the bullet hitting his father just above the sternum, a fatal shot. Vance Dingham was dead by the time he hit the floor.

Now the boys had to move fast. Their mother would be home soon. They had to hide the body before she got there. Fortunately, the siblings had been planning this for three months. They had a roll of garbage bags at the ready. Vance was unceremoniously swathed in plastic and then dragged upstairs to be hidden in the attic. The small amount of blood that had seeped through his clothes was quickly mopped up. That task was completed with just minutes to spare before Eve Dingham walked through the door. Her first action was to yell at her sons for having the stereo so loud. They'd turned it up to mask the sound of the gunshots.

Eve Dingham's stereo tirade would be the last she ever directed at her sons. The words died in her throat as she saw Jeffrey holding the gun. The boy fired three times, each bullet finding its mark. Then, as his mother collapsed to the floor, he handed off the gun to his brother. This was an agreement between them. Robert had insisted that it would be he who killed their mother. "Die, bitch," he snarled as he stood over the injured woman. Then he pulled the trigger, hitting his mom in the head and killing her. Eve's body was wrapped in a similar way to that of her husband. She ended up stashed in the basement.

With their parents dead, the Dingham brothers were free to do whatever they wanted, no rules, no curfew, certainly no yelling. Robert Dingham's first act was to raid his father's wallet and then to drive to a nearby mall to buy himself a CD player. Then he went

to visit his girlfriend to show off his purchase and to tell her that
curfews would no longer be a problem. Jeffrey, meanwhile, sat
watching TV and snacking on Doritos before going to a friend's
house to play some baseball. Over the course of the weekend, the
brothers would be seen out and about at all hours. They also
appeared to be flush with cash. When friends asked about the
sudden change, they said that their parents had gone out of town
on a spur-of-the-moment vacation.

But that story was not going to hold for very long. When Monday
came and neither Vance nor Eve showed up at work, their
colleagues became concerned about them. After failing to raise
either of them by phone, someone called the police and asked
them to check on the family. Officers arrived at the house soon
after but found the place locked up. They then tracked Robert to
his school and asked if they could carry out a search of the
property. That placed Robert in an impossible position. He could
not refuse without arousing suspicion. His only hope was that the
officers would be slipshod in carrying out their search. They were
not.

Placed under arrest and subjected to some fierce interrogation, the
siblings initially stuck together, refusing to incriminate one
another. But then prosecutors decided to offer Jeffrey Dingham a
deal and he turned on his brother. According to him, the whole
thing had been Robert's idea. He'd only gone along with the plan
because he was afraid of his older brother. He also insisted that
the bullets he'd directed at his parents had merely wounded them.
It was Robert who'd fired the kill shots, he said. In exchange for his
testimony, Jeffrey was allowed to plead to a lesser charge and to
accept a term of 30 years in prison.

Robert Dingham was now left to face the music alone. At trial, his defense team took the obvious strategy open to them. They tried to deflect the blame towards the prosecution's key witness, Jeffrey. According to this narrative, it was Jeffrey who had been the key mover, the planner, the shooter. Robert's only crimes were that he'd failed to intervene and that he'd helped to hide the bodies. It was a version of events that could not be proven but was equally difficult to disprove. The intention was to create reasonable doubt in the minds of the jurors.

Unfortunately for Robert and his team, the weight of the evidence was against them. Robert liked to talk and had been bragging to his friends for months about the murders he was going to commit. There was also physical evidence pointing to his guilt. His prints were all over the gun safe and the keys to the safe. Those keys were found hidden in his dresser drawer, along with $600 in cash, presumably stolen from his father. The prosecutor also provided an alternative motive for the murders. This wasn't about two kids defending themselves against abusive parents, he said. It was about the $200,000 that Robert Dingham wanted to inherit.

In the end, the weight of the evidence overwhelmed Dingham's reasonable doubt defense. He was found guilty and sentenced to life in prison without parole. Barring some change in the law, he will spend the rest of his days behind bars. Not so for Jeffrey. He was released on parole in 2013.

William Cornick

Ann Maguire was a much-loved teacher at Corpus Christi Catholic College in Leeds, England. The 61-year-old had been teaching Spanish at the school for nearly 41 years, her entire career. After those many years of devoted service, she was looking forward to a well-deserved retirement. She'd be calling time on her career in September 2014. Although that was still six months away, the tributes were already pouring in – from students past and present, from colleagues and former colleagues. The idea of Corpus Christi College without Ann Maguire was unthinkable, they said. She was part of the fabric of the school and would be sorely missed.

But there was one Corpus Christi student who did not share in the adulation of Ann Maguire. His name was William Cornick, and he was 15 years old and in the tenth grade. Will was just an ordinary kid who did well at school and had a good attendance record and very few disciplinary issues. Mrs. Maguire had certainly never had a problem with him. And yet, Will had developed an irrational hatred towards the Spanish teacher. He often ranted about her in Facebook messages to his friends, saying that "she deserves more than death, more than pain, and more than anything that we can understand." He even half-jokingly offered a fellow student £10 to "knock her off."

The roots of this hatred are difficult to fathom. There had only ever been one incident between teacher and student. That was when Mrs. Maguire barred Will from attending a school bowling night after he failed to hand in a Spanish assignment. The boy had attended anyway and there'd been no repercussions. In any case, that incident happened a long time after Will Cornick first expressed his loathing for Mrs. Maguire. It may have fueled the fire of what was to come, but it was not the reason for his hatred. To uncover the roots of the fixation, we have to examine William Cornick's background.

Will Cornick had been raised in a single-parent home. His parents, Ian and Michelle, were divorced when he was just four years old. Thereafter, he remained in the care of his mother, while his father remarried and fathered another son. Growing up without a dad can be difficult for a boy although Will appeared to take it in his stride. His parents remained on good terms, and he saw his father regularly and got on well with his stepmother and half-brother.

But then came an ill-fated family vacation to Cornwall in 2011. During that trip, William collapsed and had to be rushed to a local hospital. There, tests would reveal that he had Type 1 diabetes, a manageable disease but one which nonetheless requires significant lifestyle changes. It wasn't only the physical symptoms that bothered Will's mother, though. It was the changes to his mood and personality. After the initial diagnosis, the boy became depressed and surly. He began inflicting self-harm although that phase was, thankfully, short-lived. It was also around this time that Will Cornick developed his irrational hatred for his teacher, Ann Maguire.

Cornick made no secret of his feelings towards Mrs. Maguire. He frequently ranted about her in Facebook messages to his friends. But things really started to escalate in 2013. That was when Will applied to join the army and was turned down because of his medical issues. Devastated by this rejection, he took to social media to vent his anger. On Christmas Eve 2013, he sent several Facebook messages to a friend, saying that he was going to "brutally murder" Ann Maguire. The friend, who had heard Will's rants before, did not take him seriously. Other acquaintances received similar messages and formed the same impression. They knew that Will had a dark and macabre sense of humor. They thought that he was kidding. No one thought to report the threats to a parent or teacher.

And so to the morning of Monday, April 28, 2014. Will Cornick had arrived at the school in good spirits and had attended classes as normal. After the morning break, he had a class on the top floor of the building, next to Mrs. Maguire's classroom. Halfway through the lesson, he got up, left the room without asking for permission, and entered the one next door. Ann Maguire did not see him walk in. She had her back turned and was leaning over a desk, helping a student with a problem. Without saying a word, Cornick approached her from behind. Catching the eye of a female student, he gave her a wink. Then he drew a knife from his sleeve, an 8-inch kitchen knife with a razor-sharp blade.

Ann Maguire never saw what was coming. Cornick struck fast, inflicting several wounds to the teacher's throat in rapid succession. One of those sliced through the jugular vein, a fatal injury. By now, there was pandemonium in the class, with students screaming and scrambling for the exit. Mrs. Maguire also managed to make it through the door, clutching her throat as blood pulsed between her fingers. But still, Cornick wasn't done. Wading through the melee, he spotted his victim and set off after her, still clutching the blade, dripping blood. It was at this point that Susan Francis, the school's Head of Languages, arrived on the scene, alerted by screams. She immediately spotted the injured teacher, then saw the wild-eyed youth, approaching with the knife. Assessing the situation in an instant, Francis dragged Mrs. Maguire into a classroom and barred the door. "He stabbed me in the neck," the injured woman whispered hoarsely before she collapsed. By the time that emergency services arrived, she was already dead.

So what did William Cornick do after carrying out this savage attack? Did he flee the scene of the crime? Did he attempt to dispose of the murder weapon? No, he simply walked to his next class, sat down at a desk, and then showed a friend a bottle of whiskey that he'd brought to school that day, to celebrate murdering his teacher. "It's a shame I didn't get to finish the job," he said, unaware that his victim had died. He was still sitting at his desk when the police arrived.

William Cornick was arrested and charged with murder. He was held at HM Prison Hindley while he awaited trial. Since Cornick had committed the murder in front of several witnesses and since he had never denied culpability, much of the pre-trial emphasis was on determining his mental state. That would turn out to be an unpleasant experience for the psychiatrists who examined Cornick. One of them later commented that he had rarely encountered an individual as callous as the 15-year-old. Cornick showed zero remorse. In fact, he seemed to revel in his crime, telling one doctor, "I wasn't in shock. I was happy. I had a sense of pride. I still do." He then added that he knew the Maguire family would be "pissed off" with him but that everything was "just fine and dandy."

Before the dreadful crime was committed, Cornick had bragged to a friend that he could get away with murder by pleading insanity. But if that was his hope, he would be sorely disappointed. The doctors ruled him sane, culpable, and fit for trial. Left with little option, Cornick then decided to plead guilty. He probably thought that his youth would gain him a lenient sentence but again the judicial system failed to play ball. The judge was scathing in his summation, calling Cornick a coward who at 6' 2" stood over a foot taller than his slightly-built, elderly victim. He then sentenced Cornick to life in prison with a minimum tariff of 20 years. That sentence was later upheld on appeal.

Gregory Ramos

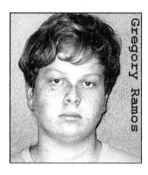

Gail Cleavenger only wanted what was best for her son, Gregory Ramos. Gregory was a bright boy but like any 15-year-old he had a lot of distractions in his life, including friends who his mother did not approve of. Recently, Gail had become concerned by the drop-off in his grades and things eventually came to a head on November 1, 2018, when Greg brought home a "D" on a school paper. Gail knew that he was capable of much better and so she took him to task about it. That sparked a furious row that had still not been resolved by the time the pair of them went to bed. Just before 11:00 p.m. that evening, Gail phoned her husband, Danny, (Greg's stepfather), and told him about the argument. Danny was away in Seattle on a business trip and told her to sleep on it. Things would look better in the morning.

The following day, Friday, November 2, Greg Ramos attended classes at University High School in Orange City, Florida. Nobody noticed anything unusual about his demeanor. But just after 4:00

p.m. that day, police in DeBary received a 911 call from an
apparently concerned Greg. He said that he had just returned to
the family home on Alicante Road and had found the place in
disarray. A door had been forced and it appeared that the house
had been ransacked. Even more alarming, his mom's SUV was
standing in the drive with the door open and the engine running.
Officers were immediately dispatched to the scene. What they
found was exactly as the boy had described.

And yet, investigators were not convinced by Greg's story.
Detectives deal with liars on a daily basis, and they usually know
when someone is trying to mislead them. Greg Ramos, in their
estimation, was doing just that. It was also easy for the officers to
discern that there had not been a burglary at the Cleavenger
residence. To their keen eyes, it was obvious that the scene had
been staged. And then there were the scratches on Greg's face that
he could not adequately explain. Greg Ramos was lying and not
even doing a very good job of it. Detectives started leaning on the
boy, pressing him to come clean about what had happened to his
mother. It didn't take long before he was talking. The testimony he
would give, and his demeanor while giving it, chilled even veteran
investigators. One detective later commented that 15-year-old
Gregory Ramos was "a soulless individual" who showed no sign of
remorse whatsoever.

According to the story told by Greg, the problem between him and
his mom had arisen over his poor grades. It had sparked an
argument, which had ebbed and flowed until around 11 p.m., when
his mother had said that she was tired and was going to bed. Greg
had retreated to his room but had found himself so annoyed by the
altercation that he was unable to sleep. He was in a rage, he said,

and had continued fuming for the next hour-and-a-half. During that time, he had decided to resolve things between him and his mother once and for all. Rising from his bed at around 12:30, he had left his room and headed down the passage. Barely pausing in the doorway, he'd stepped into his mother's darkened bedroom.

Gail Cleavenger was asleep when her son entered but was roused from slumber when he put a hand on her shoulder and shook her awake. Then, as she slowly stirred into wakefulness, Greg clamped a hand on her throat and started squeezing, cutting off her air supply. Immediately, Gail started thrashing, fighting desperately to free herself. As a martial arts black belt, she would have been no pushover. But Greg did martial arts too and he was strong for his age. Gail was also trapped under the bed covers and Greg had the element of surprise. Freeing one of her arms, Gail lashed out, raking her nails across her son's face and drawing blood. But still Greg held on, still his hands remained clamped on his mother's throat, slowly squeezing the life out of her. Gail's struggles were starting to subside. Eventually, she stopped struggling altogether; eventually, she lay still, apparently dead.

Greg Ramos had not really thought through the rest of his plan. He'd not really considered how he was going to cover up the murder. Now he had a situation. The way he saw it, there were two options. He could call the police and claim that his mom had been killed during a home invasion; or he could get rid of the body and make it look as though Gail had been abducted. Since he took a criminal justice class at school, Greg was well aware of the power of forensics. Even with his limited knowledge, he knew that the police would look for DNA evidence on the corpse. Finding none that could be linked to a third party, they'd zero in on him as a

suspect. That could not be allowed to happen. He would have to
dispose of the corpse.

With that in mind, Greg headed for the garden shed, returning a
short while later with a wheelbarrow. He arrived to a disturbing
scene. Gail was alive, gagging, trying to get up from the bed. It was
at this point that the case took a truly disturbing twist. Greg could
have abandoned his plan, gone to his mom's assistance and
revived her, taken whatever consequences were coming his way
for the attack. But he didn't do that. Instead, he clamped his hands
on her throat again, squeezing until he finished the job he'd
started. A pathologist would later estimate that it had taken the
boy 30 minutes to end his mother's life.

Gail was now loaded into the wheelbarrow, pushed out to the
drive, and unceremoniously dumped into the back of her car. Greg
had already decided on his mother's final resting place. He had
decided to bury her under a fire pit at the River City Church, about
a half-mile from the Cleavenger residence.

But this was a big job and dawn was fast approaching. Greg would
need help and for this, he called on two high school buddies, 17-
year-olds Dylan Ceglarek and Brian Porras. You might think that
kids this age would be horrified by Greg's admission that he'd
murdered his mother, reluctant to get involved, terrified of the
consequences. Apparently not. Ceglarek and Porras immediately
agreed to meet their friend at the church. There they helped dig
the narrow trench that was to be Gail Cleavenger's final resting
place. After burying the body, the three teens returned to the
house, where they forced a door, threw open some drawers, and

removed several items, in an effort to simulate a burglary. The three boys later enjoyed a celebratory soda together before going their separate ways. Now, some sixteen hours later, they were reunited. Ceglarek and Porras were rounded up and charged as accessories to murder. Greg Ramos was charged with killing his mother.

Ceglarek and Porras were just as quick as Ramos to admit their roles in the murder. They soon led detectives to the spot where they'd hidden the items they'd taken from the house, including a rifle and a PlayStation 4 console. Then they accompanied the police to the church, where Gail Cleavenger's body was found, buried just a couple of feet below the surface. Greg Ramos, it emerged, had harbored ambitions of becoming a homicide detective. Apparently, he had believed that the knowledge he'd gained in his criminal justice class would help him outfox the police. He was badly mistaken. His "perfect murder" had been solved in less than 24 hours.

Gregory Ramos was indicted as an adult for the first-degree premeditated murder of his mother, Gail Cleavenger. He entered a not guilty plea at his first court appearance but later changed his plea to guilty to avoid a life term. He was sentenced to 45 years behind bars. A detective who worked the case commented that Ramos was one of the "top three sociopaths," he'd encountered during his long career.

Shannon & Melissa Garrison & Allen Goul

Being a single mom can sometimes feel like the toughest, loneliest job in the universe. What with paying bills, putting food on the table, and running an orderly household, it must seem at times like indentured servitude. And then there is the dual mom/dad role you are required to perform in providing guidance and direction to your kids, kids who become more and more resistant to your influence as they grow up. It is hard work and often the sacrifices go unappreciated.

In the face of these challenges, Betty Garrison was doing the best that she could. Betty was a 45-year-old divorcee, raising her daughters, Shannon, 17, and Melissa, 15, in Gulfport, Mississippi during the early 90s. And she seemed to be making a good job of it. The girls were well-mannered, considerate, and sensible. Melissa, in particular, was academically gifted. Neighbors said that Betty was likable and always pleasant. One of her friends called her the "sweetest person in the world."

And yet, despite these ringing endorsements, all was not well in the Garrison household. Betty was known to be strict on her girls, perhaps too strict. Often, she'd hand down disproportionately harsh punishments for minor missteps. Melissa had recently been grounded for a month after she forgot to do a simple household chore. Shannon had been punished too, in her case for sneaking out of the house to meet her boyfriend. And these were not the only punitive measures doled out to the girls. It all led to a toxic

atmosphere developing between mother and daughters. Betty
must have been aware of this ill-feeling, but it did nothing to
change her behavior. If anything, it made her more determined to
stamp her authority on the household.

Shannon and Melissa were clearly frustrated by their mother's
autocratic rules and Shannon was quite candid about her feelings.
She spoke often about her hatred for Betty and even published a
poem in the Gulfport High School magazine, in which she gave
voice to her resentment.

My eyes were two burning embers of hatred,

My face cold and uncaring,

I laughed into your dead (silent) face,

You, it was you,

You formed me,

You pressed my sensitive soul into this mold,

I am your creation gone awry,

It looks like you got a taste,

Of your own medicine, Mommy.

In view of what was to come, this makes chilling reading. Shannon
was also prone to making bizarre claims about her participation in
witchcraft and Satanism. She once told a group of friends that it
would be "cool" to be married to a mass murderer.

Melissa Garrison was not as demonstrative as her sister. She kept her feelings mostly to herself although she did complain about her mother to her boyfriend, 15-year-old Robert Goul. It was in these conversations that a dreadful plan had its genesis.

Depending on who you believe, it was either Robert Goul who first suggested that they should murder Betty, or it was Shannon and Melissa who approached him and asked for his help in killing their mother. Whatever the truth of the matter, the three co-conspirators decided that Betty had to die and began planning how they would carry out the murder. A date was set. Tuesday, July 7, 1992, was to be Betty Garrison's last day on earth.

On the day before the murder, Shannon and Melissa received a note from Goul, outlining step-by-step instructions, including suggestions for the disposal of the body. Later that day, there was a second note, this one addressed only to Melissa. "Tonight!" it read. "Open the window at 2:30 or keep a lookout for me walking on the street. I may be a little earlier. Be ready, O.K."

If there was any chance for the sisters to pull out of their diabolical scheme it was now. And yet, neither of them did. They were determined to go through with it. Melissa was there to open the window when Goul showed up at 2:30. She led him through the house to the bedroom where Betty slept and where Shannon already waited. Shannon had a pillow in her hand, just as Goul's note had instructed. On a signal from Goul, she pounced on her mother and pushed the pillow over her face. At the same time,

Goul pinned Betty down and started stabbing her with a pocketknife he'd brought along for that purpose.

Betty fought hard for her life. She kicked and scratched and screamed. Her nails raked a path across Goul's face and chest, even as he continued stabbing her. Then she managed to wriggle free and scurried under the bed in a desperate attempt to escape her attackers. From the doorway, Melissa was screaming: "Is she dead yet? Kill her! Shut her up!" She then helped her sister in grabbing their mother's legs and pulling her out from under the bed. Then Goul resumed the attack, straddling Betty and putting his hands on her throat. Betty Garrison was slowly throttled to death while her teenage daughters watched. The last thing she heard was Shannon telling her, "Mother, you've got to die now."

Betty was dead and her killers now had the problem of either disposing of the body or coming up with a cover story. The sisters had already decided that Goul's plan for disposal was impractical and so they left the house in order to think and also to dispose of evidence. The murder weapon and several items of bloody clothing were tossed as they walked to a friend's house. After spending a while there, they went to see Shannon's boyfriend, Michael Brewer. After listening to their barely believable story, Brewer suggested that they should make it look as though Betty had been killed during a robbery. That was the plan that they went with.

Just after 6 a.m. that morning, a 911 dispatcher in Gulfport received a call from a young woman who identified herself as Shannon Garrison and said that her mother had been "hurt."

Officers immediately responded to the scene and found that Shannon had somewhat understated the case. Betty was dead. Brutally stabbed and strangled. According to the girls, they had been out visiting friends and had returned to find their mother in this condition.

But detectives were immediately suspicious of the story told by the sisters. And those suspicions only deepened when they spotted Robert Goul lurking nearby. Called over to answer questions, Goul said that he lived next door and was Melissa Garrison's boyfriend. He could provide no suitable explanation, however, for the fresh scratches on his face and chest. He and the Garrison sisters were therefore taken to the station for questioning. In the meantime, officers carried out a search and found the notes Goul had written. It all fell apart for the conspirators from there.

As the matter headed for trial, the killers turned on one another. According to Goul, the sisters had recruited him to kill their mother. Shannon, backed up by Melissa, insisted that it had been his idea all along. Those claims and counterclaims would continue until the eve of the trial. Then Shannon Garrison and Robert Goul buckled and decided to plead guilty and accept the punishments due to them – life in prison.

Melissa, meanwhile, was continuing to proclaim her innocence. Both Shannon and Goul's stories backed up her assertion that she had played no part in the actual murder but that did not absolve her of responsibility. She may not have struck any of the physical blows, but she was equally culpable. Prosecutors were determined to obtain a conviction against her and put her through three trials,

all of which ended in hung juries. Eventually, Melissa was allowed
to plead to manslaughter. She would spend just a year behind bars
before her release in 1999.

Freedom, however, would be a short-lived thing for Melissa
Garrison. Three years after her release, she contracted a lung
infection that would prove fatal. She died in June 2002 at the age of
just 25. Some would call that poetic justice.

Christopher Pittman

It was a case that put a 12-year-old on trial for a double homicide. It was also a case in which serious questions were raised about giving anti-depressants to children. Christopher Pittman had been prescribed two different SSRIs (selective serotonin reuptake inhibitors) during his short life. First Paxil (which appeared to have a positive effect) and then Zoloft which, according to his trial attorney, turned him into a cold-blooded killer.

Christopher Pittman was born on April 9, 1989, in Huntsville, Alabama. His family later moved to Oxford, Florida, where familial harmony would be in short supply. After just a couple of years in the Sunshine State, his mother abandoned the family. She later returned, only to hit the road a few weeks later, never to be seen again. Thereafter, the boy was raised by his father and developed a tense relationship with him. Christopher was a problem child and Joe Pittman was not a man of nurturing habits. He preferred to resolve disciplinary issues at the stinging end of a leather belt.

Of course, many children are raised in similarly difficult situations and most of them suffer the slings and arrows and somehow make it through. But Christopher was a sensitive boy, prone to depression and suicidal thoughts. Once, he even threatened to kill himself in front of his sister. At age 12, he twice ran away from home, resulting in his internment at a juvenile facility. There, he was examined by a child psychiatrist who determined that he was suffering from mild depression and prescribed Paxil. After Chris's discharge from the facility, Joe Pittman decided that it might be best to send the boy to live with his paternal grandparents for a while. Christopher got on well with his grandfather (also named Joe) and with his grandmother, Joy. They, in turn, adored their grandson and were happy to have him.

And so, Christopher was shipped off to South Carolina, arriving with his prescription for Paxil, a drug which appeared to have a stabilizing effect on him. Unfortunately, Paxil was not available in Chester and so a doctor there suggested substituting it with Zoloft. In theory, this makes perfect sense. Both drugs are SSRIs. In theory, they should have a similar effect on the patient.

But this wasn't the case with Christopher Pittman. Paxil had calmed him; Zoloft caused him to experience a burning sensation all over his body, a sensation so painful that he had to start taking painkillers. When this was reported to the doctor, his solution was to up the dosage from 100mg to 200mg daily. This had an even more pronounced effect on Chris. His behavior now took on a manic quality and he became argumentative and difficult. On one occasion, he caused a scene in church when he started verbally abusing the piano player. That prompted his grandparents to consider returning him to his father.

But even worse was to come just a few days later, on November 28, 2001, when Chris got into an altercation on the school bus and started throttling a younger child. Had he not been physically restrained, he might have caused serious injury to the boy. That night, the long-suffering Joe Pittman Sr. finally snapped and gave his grandson a paddling. He also told Chris that this was the last straw. He could remain in Chester no longer. He was being sent back to Florida.

Later that same night, someone placed a 911 call to the Chester County authorities, reporting that the Pittman place was on fire. Firefighters and police immediately rushed to the scene and were confronted with a fierce blaze. By the time they eventually got it under control, the house had been all but destroyed. And that wasn't even the worst of it. Inside the master bedroom lay the bodies of Joe and Joy Pittman. They had been badly burned but the fire had not completely obliterated the evidence. The Pittmans had not died in the flames. They had been blown away with a shotgun. This was now a murder inquiry.

And the police would soon learn that they had another mystery to unravel. Christopher Pittman, the couple's grandson, was missing. So too was Joe Pittman's truck and the contents of his gun cabinet. Also unaccounted for was the family dog. Had Christopher been taken by the person who had committed this atrocity or was there a more sinister explanation behind his disappearance? Was it

possible that the 12-year-old had murdered his grandparents? To
find the answer, the police would have to find Christopher.

That turned out to be easier than expected. The boy was found two
counties away, parked at the side of the road in his grandfather's
truck, having run out of gas. The family dog was with him, as was
Joe Pittman's gun collection and $33 in cash. Taken into custody,
Chris told a story about a large, black man who had entered the
house, killed his grandparents, and then lit the place on fire. He
had also tried to kidnap Chris, but he'd escaped and fled in the
truck.

It was an unconvincing account to begin with and it quickly fell
apart under interrogation. Caught in one lie too many, Christopher
changed his story. He now admitted that it was he who had killed
his grandparents and started the fire. However, it was the Zoloft
that made him do it. According to the boy, the medication caused
him to hear voices that instructed him to kill. It was as though he
was "in a dream or on a TV show," he said, aware of everything
that was happening but unable to stop it.

As the matter headed to trial, this would become the central issue
of the case. Was Christopher Pittman a heartless killer, who had
murdered his grandparents because they had threatened to send
him back to Florida? Or was he a drug-addled kid who had
committed the killings while hearing voices brought on by his
medication? Was he, as his attorney claimed, a victim of
'unintentional intoxication'?

Zoloft does indeed have side effects similar to those described by Christopher. It can cause hallucinations, paranoia, and aggressive behavior. However, the prosecutor disputed that this was what had happened here. He argued that the defense was aware of the potential effects of Zoloft and was cynically exploiting them in an attempt to have the charges reduced from murder to manslaughter. That was the way that the judge saw it too. He not only rejected the reduced charge, he also upheld the prosecution motion to try Pittman as an adult.

Christopher Pittman's long-delayed murder trial finally got underway on Monday, January 31, 2005, three years after the murders. As expected, his lawyers raised the Zoloft defense. They brought in an expert to testify as to the dangers of switching a patient from Paxil to Zoloft and yet more experts to tell the court that Zoloft should never be prescribed for someone under the age of 18. It was all to no avail. On February 15, 2005, Christopher Pittman was convicted of murder and sentenced to two concurrent terms of 30 years in prison. The conviction and sentence were later upheld on appeal.

Jamar Siler

This was a disaster waiting to happen, a tragedy waiting to unfold. The players were just children, two 15-year-olds who had endured similarly difficult paths through life and had now been set on a collision course. Still, it might never have come to this – to a cold-blooded shooting in a public place – had it not been for the stage on which the drama would play out. Central High School in Knoxville, Tennessee is an institution with a proud history. It has produced countless celebrated alumni, from well-known musicians and actors to sports stars, academics, and entrepreneurs. But at the time that our story takes place, Central High was a school in crisis, a place where unruly behavior was the norm, where fights between students were frequent, where parents fretted over the safety of their kids. There could not have been a worse environment for a troubled young man like Jamar Siler.

Jamar Siler was born in Florida in 1994. His parents were both crack cocaine addicts and his mother had used drugs throughout her pregnancy. It was no surprise when her son was later removed from her custody. But for Jamar that was barely an improvement. He was bounced from one foster home to another, always moved on when his behavior became too much for his guardians to handle. He also spent some time in juvenile hall before ending up in Lonsdale, a tough blue-collar neighborhood of Knoxville, Tennessee, in 2008. It was then that he first started attending Central High and then that he first came into contact with Ryan McDonald.

Ryan's upbringing had been startlingly similar to Jamar's. His parents, too, had problems with drugs and alcohol. Both had spent time in prison, Joey McDonald for drug-related offenses and his wife, Barbara, for prostitution. While both parents served time, Ryan was bounced between relatives until his grandmother, Genny Miller, eventually gained custody. That was a good thing for the boy, providing him with a stable home at last.

But by then, Ryan had another problem. At age three, he developed alopecia, a condition that causes the sufferer's hair to fall out. This produces no other health issues, but it did result in Ryan being teased throughout his childhood. And like many kids who are taunted and bullied, he developed a tough exterior. According to all who knew him, Ryan was a kind-hearted boy who looked out for smaller kids in the neighborhood and hoped to work as a counselor with troubled children one day. He also loved animals and regularly fed a stray dog who lived in an abandoned house in the area. Ryan, however, was no softie. He stood his ground and backed down for no one. It was this attitude that would put him into direct conflict with Jamar Siler.

We don't know for certain how the conflict between Ryan McDonald and Jamar Siler started or how it escalated. There are accounts from fellow students of an altercation on the school bus, but this appears to have been a minor incident. Jamar, who had already developed a reputation as a bully at Central High, tried to intimidate Ryan and Ryan pushed back. They were quickly separated, and no punches were thrown. This makes what happened next all the more inexplicable.

The Central High School cafeteria can be a rowdy place before classes start, with students engaged in animated conversations, goofing off, shouting out mock insults to friends and classmates. For the most part, teachers and security staff just let it be. Kids will be kids. So when the usual din was perorated by a popping sound on the morning of August 21, 2008, no one paid particular attention. Those who heard it thought that one of the kids had fired a toy gun or let off a firecracker. It was only when Ryan McDonald slumped forward, slid from his bench, and started convulsing on the floor that anyone took notice. Then someone saw the spreading rosette of blood on Ryan's chest and all hell broke loose. Kids were screaming, running every which way, scrambling for the exits. A school resource officer and a security guard responded, entering the pandemonium and spotting Ryan on the floor. A call was made to 911 and police and paramedics were soon rushing to the scene.

The first officers were at the school within minutes and ordered an immediate lockdown, in order to gain control of the situation. Two students were found who had witnessed the shooting. They said that they had seen Jamar Siler approach Ryan as he sat alone at a table. He'd reached into his rucksack and produced a gun. Without saying a word, he'd pulled the trigger, firing a single shot that hit Ryan in the chest. Then, as chaos ensued in the cafeteria, Jamar had disappeared into the crowd. He'd later been seen running from the school.

With a name and description in hand, the Knoxville police put out a bulletin, informing all units to be on the lookout for Jamar in the vicinity of the school. The boy had not gone far. He was picked up at 8:17, just three blocks from Central High. Six minutes had elapsed from the time that he'd pulled the trigger. The murder weapon, a 9mm semi-automatic pistol, was still in his possession, four bullets in the magazine. Jamar meekly handed this over to police as he was taken into custody.

While all of this was going on, Ryan McDonald had been rushed to the E.R. at UT Medical Center in Knoxville. But the bullet had caused severe damage to his internal organs. Despite the desperate efforts of doctors, Ryan didn't make it. This was now a case of murder. By 3:50 that afternoon, 15-year-old Jamar Siler had been formally charged.

What followed over the next three years was a jurisdictional battle. Initially, Siler was arraigned in juvenile court before a petition to have him tried as an adult was successful. He was now looking at the prospect of 50 years to life if found guilty. Aware of

these high-stakes, defense attorney Russell Greene started
working on a novel defense. No clear motive for the shooting had
been established. Siler and McDonald had clashed in the past, but
the nature of that clash was hardly enough to warrant a cold-
blooded execution in a school cafeteria. There had also been
suggestions that the shooting might have been racially motivated
but there was no evidence to support this. The police had even
looked into the possibility this was gang-related but again, there
was nothing to back up the theory. Despite hours of interrogation,
Siler could not, or would not, explain his actions.

Into this vacuum, Greene was getting ready to insert his own
theory. He planned to argue that Jamar had acted on an impulse
that he was unable to control. The cause of this, according to
Greene, was fetal alcohol syndrome. Siler, he claimed had suffered
brain impairment due to his mother drinking and taking drugs
while she was pregnant with him. Effectively, it was a diminished
responsibility argument.

Greene would have been aware, however, that such arguments are
difficult to sell to a jury, especially in right-leaning Tennessee,
where there is a strong law and order bias. When the prosecutor
offered a deal, he was prepared to listen. The offer on the table
was this – a guilty plea to second-degree murder in exchange for
30 years in prison, less three years for time served. After
discussing it with his client, Greene accepted.

And so, Jamar Siler shuffled off to begin serving a sentence that
will see him spend the prime of his life behind bars. His
unwarranted and inexplicable act had snuffed out the life of a child

his own age. Siler will pay his debt to society by forfeiting his own youth.

Todd Smith

On the morning of April 20, 1999, two heavily armed high school seniors entered the cafeteria at Columbine High School in Colorado and opened fire on their fellow students. They then rampaged through the school building, shooting at anyone they encountered. By the time Eric Harris and Dylan Klebold were done, twelve students and one teacher lay dead. The pair then added to the carnage by committing suicide. It was, at the time, the deadliest school shooting in US history.

The massacre at Columbine sent shockwaves reverberating around the world. Nearly one thousand miles away, in the small town of Taber, in Alberta, Canada, it attracted the particular attention of 14-year-old Todd Cameron Smith. Todd had little in common with the Columbine shooters, Harris and Klebold. They had been disaffected, malevolent individuals, intent on leaving their malign mark on the world. He was shy, socially awkward, and reclusive, a solitary kid without a friend in the world.

And yet, Todd identified strongly with Harris and Klebold. He identified with their anger, with their sense of isolation. He identified with their desire to hit back at a system that had let them down. In Todd's case, there was at least some basis for that anger. Sensitive and intelligent, he had been the victim of severe bullying since his first day at school. This had continued into high school and went way beyond the occasional wedgie and having his head dunked in a toilet bowl. In one horrific incident, someone had doused Todd with lighter fluid and threatened to strike a match. It had left the boy anxious and fearful. He began to suffer from depression and started to self-harm. He developed a taste for extreme death metal music as an outlet for his anger. He lost himself for hours on end, browsing the internet. Eventually, in early 1999, he dropped out and stopped attending W.R. Myers High School. Raised in a strict Mormon home, he was being home schooled by his parents.

Now, though, as Todd sat compulsively watching the horrific footage emerging from Colorado, he felt strangely at peace. A plan had begun to ferment in his mind, the culmination of every revenge fantasy he had ever harbored. The Columbine shooters had shown the courage to strike back at those who stood against them. Did he have the guts to do the same? He believed that he did.

School shootings are rare in Canada, at least when compared to the frequency of such events in its southern neighbor. Gun control legislation is far stricter than in the US and socio-economic conditions are less conducive to these acts of wanton violence. In fact, there had not been a single incident at a Canadian secondary school since the late 1970s. But that was to change on Wednesday, April 28, 1999. Just eight days after Harris and Klebold's infamous rampage at Columbine, Todd Smith arrived at W.R. Myers High School intent on murder.

The Columbine shooters had spent months planning their attack and had brought plenty of firepower, a large cache of ammunition, even pipe bombs. Todd Smith was not so meticulous. He was carrying a .22-caliber rifle, the barrel cut down so that it could be concealed under his blue trench coat. He did not have a specific plan, only the intention to shoot the first person he encountered. Since he had entered the school building just after the lunch break, those were few and far between. The students had just begun afternoon classes. But then Smith did spot someone, a female teacher who he recognized walking directly towards him. Removing the rifle from his coat, he shouldered it and took aim. The teacher was in his sights. He tightened his finger on the trigger.

But now there occurred a truly remarkable incident. Seeing the boy with the rifle pointed at her, the teacher issued a sharp reprimand. She told the boy to quit fooling around and to leave the school premises at once. Amazingly, Todd Smith obeyed, lowered his weapon, turned on his heel, and skulked out the way he'd come. It might all have ended right there had Jason Lang and Shane Christmas not been late returning to class that day.

Lang and Christmas were two of Todd Smith's old nemeses. Now, seeing Smith headed towards them, they could not resist one final jibe. It was a fatal error. Smith immediately produced the rifle and unleashed a barrage of bullets. Lang was hit in the neck, while Christmas took a round in the stomach. Another boy who was with them, had a narrow escape. He was grazed by a stray bullet. It might have been even worse had gym teacher Cheyno Finnie not arrived at that moment and tackled Smith to the ground. The shooter was then marched to the administrative office where he was held until the police arrived.

Todd Smith had fallen considerably short of his aim of creating another Columbine at W.R. Myers High. But the results of his shooting spree were nonetheless devastating. Jason Lang, just 17, was dead at the scene. His friend, Shane Christmas, had been rushed to hospital where his chances of survival were rated 50-50. Christmas would eventually make a full recovery. Smith, however, still had one count of first-degree murder to answer to, plus two counts of attempted murder.

The W.R. Myers shootings instilled a sense of deep shock among Canadians, many of whom believed that their strict gun control laws immunized them against such occurrences. There had, of course, been the infamous École Polytechnique massacre in Montreal a decade earlier but that had occurred on a university campus. No one expected something like this at a high school. Even the legal system was thrown into a quandary. Should Smith be tried as an adult or was this a matter for the youth authorities? In the end, it was decided that the case would be heard in juvenile court. That was good news for Smith. Rather than facing the prospect of life in prison, he was looking at a maximum term of five years.

Before the matter came before the court, however, there would be yet another dramatic twist. Todd Smith was found to be suffering from a heart condition that required immediate surgery. During the procedure, he suffered a stroke and lapsed into a coma. When he emerged from that state, he had difficulty speaking and appeared to have diminished mental capacity. It was thought at this time that the trial might have to be abandoned but then Smith staged a recovery that doctors described as "miraculous." By September 2000, he was ready to appear in court.

Todd Smith entered a guilty plea at trial and received the expected sentence – five years in a juvenile facility plus an additional seven years on probation after his release. He was released in March 2005, despite warnings that he still presented a threat to society.

In August of that year, the now 20-year-old Smith walked away from a halfway house in Toronto, leaving behind a note that read: "I won't be caged any longer. Next time, I won't surrender." The discovery of this note sparked panic. There were genuine fears that Smith was planning another massacre. Police in Toronto were placed on full alert and a massive manhunt was launched for the fugitive. Smith, whose name and image had been withheld from the public during his original trial, now saw his picture splashed across the front page of every newspaper in the country. Fortunately, the crisis was averted. With every cop in the country looking for him, Todd Smith surrendered himself to the authorities the next day.

Danielle Black

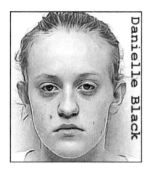

It is a situation that parents of teenagers are all too familiar with. Their teen hits puberty and is suddenly transformed from an obedient, loving kid into a rebel who seems at war with the world. Reasonable parental instructions become a rallying call for insurrection, grades slip, curfews are ignored, the child starts hanging out with friends who fall under the parental catchall of "bad influence." If you've ever raised a teenaged son or daughter, you can probably relate. The parents of 15-year-old Danielle Black would certainly have sympathized.

Danielle was, in many ways, a poster child for teenage rebellion. Growing up in a stable, middle-class home in Hagerstown, Maryland, she was raised to be a caring child. She was close to her father, Billy, and got on well with her stepmom, Andrea. She did well academically and was never a problem to her teachers. She had a close relationship with her older brother, Justin. But then Danielle entered her sophomore year at high school and all of that changed. Suddenly, she had adopted the Goth culture and was dressing all in black, wearing corpse-like makeup and painting her fingernails a deep shade of magenta. She was also drinking, doing drugs, and sleeping around. Her grades plummeted and she developed disciplinary problems at school. And that wasn't even the worst of it. Danielle started self-harming, cutting herself and drinking her own blood.

For Billy Black, this was a nightmare scenario. His beloved daughter was slipping away from him and it seemed there was nothing he could do to turn things around. Grounding didn't work, and neither did docking his daughter's allowance. Curfews and other disciplinary measures were equally ineffective. So too was the conciliatory approach. Danielle would listen to her father's pleas and exhortations in brooding silence and then continue as before. She began to resent what she saw as his efforts to control her. To friends, she professed that she hated him. She even started to fantasize about killing him.

Those who knew Billy Black spoke of him in glowing terms. He was, according to one acquaintance, an "uncommonly good man." But now Danielle began to trash his reputation. She started spreading nasty rumors among her group of friends, claiming that her father beat her, that he brutalized her psychologically, that he sexually molested her. These lies did not fall on fallow ground. One young man, in particular, took them on board...and they made him angry.

Alec Scott Eger (or Alec Scott Raven, as he preferred to call himself) was part of the group of Goths that Danielle Black hung out with. At 19, he was slightly older than the others and saw himself as a sort of guardian to them. He went by the self-applied nickname, 'The Protector,' and this was more to him than just a nifty handle. Eger was from a broken home and had suffered horrific sexual abuse in childhood. His mission in life was to prevent the same thing from happening to other kids. This was explicitly laid out in the About Me section of his Myspace page:

"The only thing left is the need for vengeance against those who cause pain, sorrow. People get away with things they should never have done yet no one punishes them. Killers, child molesters, rapists, wife-beaters, etc. So the question I ask is this. Is it wrong to exact vengeance on those who deserve it, in defense and revenge for those who cannot protect themselves? Because in this world of unjust ignorance you are the only one who will stand up for those who need help."

Given this mission statement, it is easy to see how Eger would have been deeply affected by Danielle's stories of abuse. Being the manipulative individual that she was, Danielle seized on this, really laying it on thick, sparing no horrific detail. She was priming the pump or, more aptly, loading the gun. If Alec Eger could be considered a weapon, Danielle Black was filling the chamber with bullets, flicking the safety off, placing her finger on the trigger. In no time at all, she had convinced Alec that the only way to end her torment was to murder her father.

On the morning of October 31, 2008 – Halloween morning – 47-year-old Billy Black left his West Hagerstown duplex to make his usual commute to work. This day, however, would be different. On

122 Robert Keller

this day, Black had not yet reached his truck when he found himself confronted by a disheveled, wild-eyed young man. He was just about to ask the stranger if he could help when the man suddenly drew a knife and attacked. Caught entirely by surprise, Black never stood a chance. Of the twenty blows that were struck, about half sliced through Billy's hands and forearms, as he tried to protect himself. But it was the rest of the knife thrusts that did the damage, landing in the neck, chest, and shoulders, severing vital blood supply lines. Billy Black bled out even as his killer dragged him into an adjacent alley, lifted his wallet, and fled. The entire episode had been witnessed by Billy's daughter, watching silently and impassively from her bedroom window.

At first, the police thought that this was a mugging gone wrong. But then they began to hear whisperings. Danielle had spoken openly about her desire to kill her father and had even tried to recruit some of her classmates at South Hagerstown High School in a murder-for-hire scheme. Someone also reported a rather callous remark she'd made at her father's funeral. "Now I can laugh, but I have to behave myself for a while," she'd been heard to comment. And then there were her writings, including a poem which seemed to hint at her father's imminent death. "Just understand if you do it again; you won't have a life to live; your days would be numbered; your ass would be gone."

With investigators now looking anew at the evidence, with even Danielle's stepmother describing her as a "cold-hearted person," detectives started questioning her Goth friends and were soon directed to 'The Protector,' Alec Scott Eger. Eger was brought in for interrogation and made no bones about his involvement in the murder. He confessed right away and told the investigators that he was proud of what he'd done and that he would do it again. He had rid the world of an abuser and child molester. Where the law had failed to act, he had stepped up.

What Eger didn't know yet, what he would soon find out, was that he had been duped. Not a shred of evidence could be found to support Danielle's allegation of abuse. In fact, the opposite was true. Billy Black had been a caring and diligent father. His only crime was that he had tried to keep his wayward daughter on the straight and narrow. That had sometimes called for tough love and had led to Danielle building up a seething resentment towards her father. That resentment had led, ultimately, to his death.

Both Alec Eger and Danielle Black were arrested and charged, he with first-degree murder; she with solicitation of first-degree murder. At Eger's trial, his defense pointed out that he was suffering from Post-Traumatic Stress Disorder due to the abuse inflicted on him in childhood. That would have made him an easy mark for someone as cunning as Danielle Black. "She is the instigator and the Charlie Manson behind her father's death," lawyer Jerome Joyce told the court, and even the prosecution witnesses seemed to agree. A detective, called to the stand, stated his opinion that Eger would never have committed murder but for Danielle's intervention. None of this did Alec Eger any good. He was sentenced to life in prison.

Now it was the turn of Danielle Black to face her day in court. In 2012, she struck a deal with prosecutors, entering a guilty plea to solicitation to commit first-degree murder and accepting a life sentence, of which all but six years were suspended.

Alec Eger is currently serving his time at Patuxent Correctional Institution, a facility in Jessup, Maryland, which houses prisoners with mental health issues. Danielle Black, meanwhile, is a free woman. She was released in 2015 having served less than four years behind bars for her brutal act of parricide.

Evan Savoie & Jake Eakin

On the rainy afternoon of February 15, 2003, there was a knock at the door of the trailer occupied by the Sorger family in Ephrata, Washington. Lisa Sorger went to answer it and found two boys on her doorstep. They wanted to know if her son, Craig, could come out and play. Lisa wasn't keen on the idea at first. Craig had learning disabilities and mild autism and she was protective of him. But Craig clearly knew the boys, who he described as "school friends." He begged his mom to be allowed out and eventually, Lisa relented, telling him to keep dry and to be home before it turned dark. Craig promised that he would be, hugged his mom, and then headed down the path with his friends.

But Craig wasn't home by the time darkness fell, he wasn't home for dinner, and he did not answer Lisa's calls when she went looking for him. Lisa then learned that the two boys he'd been playing with had long since returned home and that was when she decided to call the police. Soon a search was underway and, just as soon, it was tragically resolved. Craig was found in a clearing among the trees, partially covered with leaves. He had been beaten and stabbed to death.

The obvious place for the police to begin their investigation was to speak to Craig's young playmates, Evan Savoie and Jake Eakin. The two 12-year-olds were questioned that very night but could add nothing that the police did not already know. According to the boys, they'd spent the afternoon playing tag and climbing trees before heading home at around 4:30. They'd left Craig on a path and had last seen him walking in the direction of his trailer. They had not seen anything out of the ordinary and had no idea what had happened to their friend. With no reason to doubt their story, the police let them go.

But the following morning, Evan's mother, Holly Parent, noticed something unusual. Her son had left his sneakers in the bathroom, and they were soaked through, as though they had been submerged in water. Holly immediately confronted Evan and demanded to know what had happened in the woods. Evan then dropped his head and said that he needed to talk to her and his stepfather, Andy Parent. He then told a revised story of what had happened to Craig. He said that Craig had fallen while they were climbing a tree. He and Jake had then scrambled down to check on the boy and had found that he wasn't breathing and that he had blood on him. Some of that blood got onto Evan's clothing as he was checking for a pulse. Believing that he would be blamed for Craig's death, Evan had jumped into a pond to wash the blood off his clothing. That was how his shoes got wet. He also said that he had left his bloodstained sweatshirt under the water, weighed down by a rock.

Holly Parent was fully prepared to accept her son's revised telling
of events. The police, however, were not. What Evan was saying
simply did not tally with the autopsy results. These showed that
Craig Sorger had been subjected to a quite horrific assault. The
child had suffered sixteen separate blunt trauma wounds to the
neck and head, a severe fracture to the base of the skull, and 34
knife wounds to the head, neck, and torso. Despite their
protestations of innocence, Evan Savoie and Jake Eakin found
themselves charged with first-degree murder and taken into
custody. With bail set at $1 million each, they were going to have
to remain behind bars while they awaited trial.

The case against Evan Savoie was strengthened even further when
his t-shirt was submitted for forensic analysis and bloodstains
returned a match for Craig's DNA. However, Evan's legal team
believed that this could be easily explained away. They suggested
that the blood had transferred to Evan while he was checking on
Craig after the fall. Thereafter Evan and Jake had left, believing
that their friend was dead. Then someone else had come along,
found the unconscious Craig, and stabbed him to death.

It was a tenuous story at best but one that any half-competent
defense attorney could have used at trial to create reasonable
doubt. And, with the right jury, it might well have resulted in an
acquittal. But divisions were now starting to appear between the
two accused. Jake had changed his story, saying that he wasn't
even present when Craig fell. He now claimed that he had gone to
buy a soda and had returned to find Craig lying dead on the

ground. Evan had convinced him to lie, he said, and he'd gone along with it to help his friend.

This new story was a rather obvious attempt by Jake to minimize his involvement and left the police more convinced than ever of his guilt. Detectives had, in the interim started looking into the backgrounds of the boys, hoping to find something that might explain their murderous actions. What they found instead was two normal kids who had nothing but minor infractions on their school records. Jake was learning disabled and barely able to read and write but he was described as a pleasant boy who was sometimes picked on because of his size. Evan was a popular kid who was known as the class clown. Neither boy appeared to have a particular interest in violent movies, video games, or music. The only item that suggested something amiss was an essay penned by Jake, in which he praised the Washington D.C. snipers, describing them as his "idols."

As the matter headed for court, the decision was announced that the boys would be tried as adults, a ruling that meant a possible 35 years behind bars if found guilty. Jake Eakin, in particular, appeared rattled by the prospect, commenting that he'd be older than his dad when he got out. This suggested an opening to prosecutors, and they took it, offering Jake a deal – his testimony against Evan in exchange for a reduced charge of second-degree murder and a recommendation of leniency. As expected, Jake, his parents, and counsel, immediately jumped on the offer.

And so, the truth of what had happened to Craig Sorger on that rainy February afternoon was finally revealed. According to Jake,

Evan had arrived at his house that day and asked him to play at a
local park. Once there, Evan had shown him a knife and told him
that he "wanted to go on a killing spree." They had then walked to
Craig Sorger's trailer and had invited him to play with them. Their
games had taken them to a nearby canal and then into the woods,
where Evan had suggested that they build a fort. He'd picked out a
spot amongst the trees and told Craig to kneel and place his palms
on the ground so he could determine if it was dry. "Hold your
hands on the ground and count to ten," Evan had said. "That's the
only way it will work. Craig had dutifully started counting, "one,
two, three..." He was only halfway through when Evan picked up a
rock "as big as a basketball" and dropped in on his neck.

Craig sprawled face down in the dirt. Almost immediately, Evan
was on him, striking him repeatedly. Jake could see blood on
Craig's neck. He couldn't see the knife but realized that Evan must
be stabbing the boy. Craig was crying out, "Why are you doing this
to me?" According to Jake, he tried to intervene, but Evan pushed
him away. Craig then tried to get up, but Evan tackled him to the
ground and continued stabbing him. Eventually, Craig lay still,
whimpering: "I'm dying, I'm dying." Then Evan turned on Jake,
calling him a "faggot" for not joining in the attack. Stung by this,
Jake picked up a stick and started hitting the badly injured boy
with it, landing blows to his head and legs. When the stick broke,
he picked up another and continued the assault, eventually landing
more than 20 blows. Finally, he dropped the weapon and Evan
then walked up to him and shook his hand.

Having committed this brutal murder, the two 12-year-olds
walked to a nearby pond and washed the blood from their hands,
faces, and clothing. They then walked home, rehearsing their cover

story as they did. They would claim that they had played with Craig and then left him to make his way home. They would claim that Craig was alive and well when they walked away from him. Had they stuck to this version of events, they might well have gotten away with it.

Jake Eakin would tell this same story at his friend's 2006 trial. It left the jury with little doubt as to Evan Savoie's culpability and resulted in a guilty verdict and a 26-year prison term, the maximum for a juvenile offender. By then, Jake Eakin had already had his day in court and had received an unpleasant surprise. Given his co-operation, the prosecutor had asked for leniency and had recommended an eight-year sentence. The judge had ignored that recommendation and imposed the maximum – 14 years behind bars.

In the years since the murder, Jake Eakin has accepted responsibility for the part he played in Craig Sorger's death and has apologized to the Sorger family. Evan Savoie, meanwhile, continues to assert that he was wrongly convicted. He has his staunchest ally in his mother, Holly Parent. "My son is innocent," Holly proclaimed to an interviewer. "The real killer is still out there."

David Biro

He chose the house because it was directly across the road from a police station. All the better to brag about. The people who lived in that house were irrelevant, pawns in a game of his design. He wanted to know what it felt like to kill someone. It was their bad luck that he'd happened to zone in on their residence.

Richard and Nancy Langert had just received wonderful news. The couple hadn't been married long when a trip to the doctor revealed that they were about to start the family that they longed for. Nancy was three months pregnant. Hardly able to wait before sharing the happy news, Nancy nonetheless kept it to herself. Glad tidings like this should be shared in an appropriate setting. And so, she and Richard invited her parents to dinner at a restaurant that night, April 7, 1990. There, they were finally able to reveal their joyous secret. For Nancy, it was the happiest night of her life. It would also be her last.

When Richard and Nancy arrived home that night, a killer was waiting for them. The assassin had broken into the couple's townhouse, in Winnetka, Illinois, using a glass cutter to remove a windowpane. He'd then pulled up a chair and waited patiently for the couple to return. When they did, he emerged from the shadows pointing a .357 magnum and threatening to shoot unless they did exactly what he said. Richard tried to reason with the man, offering him money if he would just leave and not harm them. But the man wasn't interested. He handed over a pair of handcuffs and ordered Richard to snap them on his wrists. Then he hustled the terrified couple down to the basement, where he forced Richard to his knees. Ignoring the couple's pitiful entreaties, he placed the gun against the back of Richard's head and pulled the trigger.

The .357 magnum is a powerful weapon. Fired at that range, into the back of a human brain, it causes massive trauma. Richard was dead before he spilled, face-first, into the concrete floor. Now the killer turned his attention to Nancy, who was cowering in the corner of the room. "Please don't kill me," she begged. "Please don't kill my baby." The killer simply ignored these cries for mercy. He pointed the gun and fired, hitting Nancy in the belly. The bullet ripped through flesh and struck the tiny fetus within, totally annihilating it. When the autopsy was conducted later on, the pathologist was not even able to determine the gender of the unborn child.

With his victims now bleeding out on the basement floor, the killer calmly pocketed his weapon, climbed the stairs, and left by the front door. He believed that he'd killed both Richard and Nancy, but he was wrong. Nancy was still alive, in terrible pain, but still breathing. She must have known, though, that she was severely injured. She didn't have much time. Using what was left of her strength, she dipped a finger into her own blood and used that to draw a symbol on the floor, a heart followed by the letter U. "I love you," a final poignant message to her family. That done, she dragged herself slowly across the floor to where her husband lay and died beside him.

The horrific murder of a much-loved couple and their unborn child sent ripples of fear and outrage through Winnetka. The police were determined to catch the killer, but their pursuit was doomed from the very start. How do you solve a murder when there is no apparent motive? How do you catch a killer who leaves behind not a single clue? Perhaps by looking at a suspect who you would never have considered.

David Biro was 16 years old and a junior at New Trier High School. He was an unusual kid, a pale, gangly loner with an oddball sense of humor and a tough guy act. He liked to wear his hair slicked back and he had a crude tattoo on his arm that he liked to show off. In fact, Biro liked to show off in general. At the time of the Langart murders, he was running for senior class president, in a campaign that seemed to most of his peers like an elaborate hoax. His campaign poster billed him as "David Biro: America's Most Wanted." During one election rally, he reportedly asked the audience, "Who do I have to blow to get elected?"

Biro had another claim to fame that spring. When he wasn't running his sham election campaign, he was making claims about a double homicide that he'd committed, boasting that he'd gotten away with it because the police were too dumb to catch him.

Although he never said it out loud, friends and classmates assumed that he was talking about the Langert killings. Nobody, however, took him seriously. They knew that Biro liked to shock. Perhaps they'd have paid more attention had they known something about his history. Some years earlier, David Biro had been confined to a psychiatric hospital, after he'd tried to poison his parents.

Six months had passed with no progress in the Langert murder inquiry. Then, in the fall of 1990, the Winnetka police received a call from a New Trier High School student. The boy had an interesting story to tell about a fellow athlete on the cross-country team. He said that the team often did a practice run that passed the townhouse where the Langerts had been killed. During one of those runs, a teammate, David Biro, had pointed out the house to him and said, "I did it." Biro had "confessed" to the killings before, of course, but something in his expression on this particular day had spooked his teammate. After mulling what to do overnight, the boy had decided to report the incident to the police.

The idea that a 16-year-old could have committed such a horrific crime seemed highly unlikely to the police. But they had little else to go on and so they brought David Biro in for questioning. And it wasn't long before the juvenile killer was talking, describing his horrific acts in gleeful detail. Explaining his motive for the killings, Biro said that he'd always wanted to know what it felt like to take a life. He'd chosen the Langert residence because he often passed it on his cross-country route and because it was directly across from the police station. He also told the police where they could find the murder weapon. It was hidden in a drawer in his bedroom.

David Biro had been four weeks shy of his 17th birthday on the night of the murders, making him a juvenile under the law. However, the state of Illinois decided to try him as an adult. That rendered him eligible for a sentence of life without parole and that is exactly what he got – two terms of life for the murders of Richard Langert and Nancy Langert, plus an additional life term for murdering their unborn child.

A life term must seem like an incredibly harsh sentence when you begin serving it as a teenager, especially when there is no possibility that you will ever qualify for parole. However, there was hope for David Biro in 2014, as the US Supreme Court ruled that the sentence constituted "cruel and unusual punishment" when imposed on a juvenile. The new law was applied retrospectively, meaning that Biro would be eligible for a new sentencing hearing, one that would set a reasonable parole period.

Unfortunately for Biro, a Cook County judge saw it differently. While Biro was granted a new hearing for the murders of the two adults, the intentional homicide of an unborn child was not covered by the Supreme Court ruling. Biro's sentence of life without parole would stand in that case. It means that he will never be released from prison.

For more True Crime books by Robert Keller please visit

http://bit.ly/kellerbooks

Printed in Great Britain
by Amazon

79309379R00078